Strengthen Your Brothers

Strengthen Your Brothers

Letters of Encouragement from an Archbishop to His Priests

J. Peter Sartain

Foreword by Francis Cardinal George, OMI

LITURGICAL PRESS
Collegeville, Minnesota

www.litpress.org

Library of Congress Control Number: 2012949752

ISBN 978-0-8146-3427-1

To

Reverend Monsignor Charles W. Elmer, PA

loving father and faithful friend to many priests

1923–2011

di cuore

"Simon, Simon, behold Satan has demanded to sift all of you like wheat, but I have prayed that your own faith may not fail; and once you have turned back, you must strengthen your brothers."

Luke 22:31-32

Contents

PRIESTLY PRAYER

Foreword

Planning is an industry now. Planners are involved in many events and are part of many movements and enterprises: wedding planners, city planners, financial planners, and many others. Planning means we take rational control of our lives, our projects, our events. It's a sign that we are responsible.

When God enters our lives, he asks us to give up control, to surrender our lives to his plan for us and for the world. It is hard to give up our plans, even when our control turns out to be illusory. It's harder still to give up our plans when God doesn't seem to have any plan we can recognize. Fifty years ago, when Pope John XXIII convoked the Second Vatican Council, he described the world as "lost, confused, and anxious" (*Humanae salutis*, December 25, 1961). So who's in charge?

Throughout Archbishop Sartain's book, there is a deep sense of God's providence, of his care for the world that he governs through the quiet working of truth and love in the midst of our sinfulness and its consequences for the world of nature and of history. Archbishop Sartain has confidence that God is in charge, because he knows in faith that truth and love are the only consistent bases for taking responsibility for others. God's governance is real and effective, even when not immediately evident.

God has placed ordained priests in charge of the Church; and the archbishop's own experience of gently governing God's people has convinced him of the efficacy of priests and their ministry. As Fathers in God, priests are to model in the Church the providential concern that God has for his Church and all his creation. Theirs is a ministry based entirely on truth and love, a ministry often expressed in small gestures, in a quiet unassuming word, in a silent presence.

In prayer, the archbishop reminds us, we recognize "that God keeps vigilant watch over us." In ministry, priests cooperate with God in caring for his people. They go from prayer to people and back again, always in company with Christ and with their brother priests. Gradually, priests come to trust the Lord with whom they habitually live and learn that self-surrender is the surest way to come to understand the ways of the Lord.

The spiritual life of the priest may be hindered by discouragement, by sin, by loss of fervor. Each of these and many other obstacles to self-surrender can serve to weaken a priest's union with Christ. Time and again, however, people's love for their priests calls the priest out of his own concerns and identifies him with the people Christ has given him to govern in love. Listening to priests speak about their parishioners is a happy experience, one for which bishops are grateful not only because they learn about their people but because they also learn about their priests. No priest is ordained without a title that tells him and the world to which people he belongs. Listening to parishioners speak about their priests confirms that identity.

The media image of the Catholic priest today is far from what it was fifty years ago. We have gone from Barry Fitzgerald to sex offender in a period that was supposed to be marked by a new springtime for the Church after the Second Vatican Council. Perhaps, in the providence of God, a great trial is necessary before it is clear that God is in charge. The priesthood is part of the constitution of the Church, a source of stability and continuity that draws fire from those who, for whatever reason, would like to see the Church retire into private experience or even disappear entirely. No matter the sins of priests and bishops, Christ governs his people, making use of priests who have come to trust him.

This book is an invitation to trust, made by an archbishop who loves his priests. It is a beautiful book, limpid and transparent in its purpose. Archbishop Sartain moves easily between personal experience and spiritual insight, strengthening the priests who will read this book. I hope many will do so.

Francis Cardinal George, OMI
Archbishop of Chicago
Feast of the Epiphany, 2012

Dedication

Out of the blue, late in the afternoon of Saturday, November 18, 1999, I received an encouraging and affirming, but uncharacteristically puzzling, e-mail from a close friend, Charlie Elmer. I was pastor of St. Louis Church in Memphis at the time, and the e-mail arrived just moments before I was to officiate a marriage. A brother priest was to concelebrate the wedding Mass, and by coincidence Charlie was also his close friend, but I chose not to mention the e-mail to him.

Charles W. Elmer was born May 19, 1923, in Aurora, Wisconsin, one of four children of John and Eva (whom Charlie always affectionately called "Mum"). The family moved to Iron Mountain, Michigan, where his parents owned a general store, above which they made their home. After graduating from Iron Mountain High School in 1941, Charlie attended the University of Wisconsin until the United States entered World War II. He joined the US Army in 1942 as part of the 430th Anti-Aircraft Battalion of the Second Armored Division. He was among the thousands of soldiers who stormed Omaha Beach in the famed D-Day invasion of Europe on June 6, 1944, and later fought in the Battle of the Bulge. He would eventually earn the rank of Colonel in the Army Reserve.

Not long before he died, he told another priest friend that, returning to the States after the war, he boarded a train in Washington for the long ride to Iron Mountain and heard the popular song, "Sentimental Journey," playing repeatedly. Listening to the line "Gonna set my heart at ease," he knew that his heart would not be at ease until he responded to the persistent urgings of Christ to become a priest. He entered St. Francis de Sales Seminary in Milwaukee and, after graduation, the North American College in Rome. Ordained a priest of the Diocese of Marquette on December 20, 1952, he transferred to the warmer climate of the Diocese of Austin due to asthma, a condition that dogged him the rest of his life. At heart a parish priest, he served several parishes and led the campus ministry program at St. Mary Parish of Texas A&M University. The majority of his years as a priest, however, were spent in the formation of priests, as Assistant Superior of the Casa Santa Maria of the North American College, Business Manager of the North American College, Director of the Casa Santa Maria and the Office of US Visitors to the Vatican, spiritual director then rector of Holy Trinity Seminary in Dallas, and spiritual director at St. Mary's Seminary in Houston.

Charlie could have chosen any path in life, so great were his gifts, but God chose him to be a priest. As all of us have turning points in life, Charlie had one of his under the inspiration of St. Rita of Cascia. I was one of many invited to accompany him on his regular pilgrimages to Cascia and the shrine of St. Rita. He and I once concelebrated Mass with the local bishop and other priests, then Charlie prayed his private prayers. He told a friend that it had been at Cascia many years earlier that the Lord had given him the choice of prestige or the spiritual influence of young men. He said that choosing the latter had been the most freeing experience of his life, one that confirmed that God had called him to be a priest to help young laymen and young priests to be holy.

I came to know him in the summer of 1974, when I began my studies at the North American College. He was the *economo* (business manager) at the time, and it was clear from our first meeting that he loved seminarians and priests. The friendship which began that summer lasted the remainder of his life, until the Lord called him home September 4, 2011. I was only one of an army of priestly "sons" whom Charlie encouraged and fathered with great love, humility, directness, and humor. Indeed, though there were literally hundreds of us, each was made to feel that he was the fair-haired one, the dearest of all. We sons joked with him about that knack of his, and he never denied having it. He took us seriously—he took our vocation seriously—and we were better priests for his loving attention and his prayers. To the end, he made himself available to seminarians and priests for counsel, compassion, and confession.

We sons were as different from one another as any large group of seminarians and priests could be, yet Charlie related to each with ease, and we with him. At his funeral, some of us compared notes. He had never been one to speak at length about his past, but occasionally he would let slip the hint of a fascinating experience or life lesson.

For instance, when I returned to the seminary from a trip to the great Cathedral at Chartres one year, I gave him an enthusiastic account of the visit. He added quietly, "The first time I was at Chartres, it was June,

1944, and I was carrying a rifle, holding up behind the Cathedral." On another occasion, when he visited me at the parish in Memphis, we went to see the movie *Platoon*. On the ride back to the rectory, he was unusually quiet. As we pulled into the driveway, he said, "I had forgotten how terrible war is."

It was clear that, even though each of us knew him well, it was in speaking of him together that we learned not only of the scope of his life experience but especially of his constancy and integrity. He was not secretive but humbly guarded, and I suppose he shared with each of us what he thought would be helpful. I was the recipient of his fatherly care on occasions too numerous to recount here. He was always interested in what I was doing and how it was going. Suffice it to say that I knew he accompanied me along the priestly journey, and he was always available to guide, challenge, and encourage. There was no mistaking the fact that he loved Jesus and his Mother with all his heart, and he gave unwavering witness to the importance of being faithful to prayer.

He was tall, lean, and straight as an arrow his entire life. He ate sparingly, loved to play tennis, and enjoyed a daily, early-morning, brisk walk through Rome; it was my joy to take many walks with him through the city and its environs. During those walks we talked of serious things that mattered and frivolous things that made us laugh. Even when in his later years he slowed and stooped with the discomfort of age, he was in a deeper sense still tall and straight, a fit ascetic. He owned little, lived simply, and shared generously. He disliked the spotlight but would not hesitate to speak publicly and with determined animation of the priesthood and his love for Christ and the Church. He could appear severe, but only momentarily, because a broad, mischievous smile inevitably emerged to unmask any appearance of sternness. He was the epitome of fatherly hospitality. Even those who met him only once knew they had met a man of depth and prayer, a man of kindness and generosity, a shepherd like Jesus, a priest thoroughly.

It was not unusual to receive emails from him, and they were often humorous, but never had they been puzzling like the one I received November 18, 1999:

> Dear Peter: This will probably seem like an odd letter but I wanted to say a few things. First off, I want to say that you have meant a lot to me through the years. You have a special place in my heart and you are as close as I will ever [be] to having a son. Distance and time have a way of keeping us separated but never in prayer. You have

been much on my mind lately as I know a lot is happening in the Church. I guess what I want to say is to be open to the Lord's call wherever and whenever that may be. Always remember that the Lord will never let you be more generous to Him than He is to you. I have generally found that for me God's will is found in the voice of the Church and especially so if I haven't been searching for a job and especially if I would rather be left alone. Each of us is asked to carry his own cross which is as different for each of us as we are different from one another. It is in the carrying of that cross that we find our own salvation. Because our God is a God who is called LOVE, we can do nothing better in our lives than to love. It is so very important that as a pastor you have a special love for your flock—even more important is the love that a Bishop must have for his flock and above all for his priests with whom he shares his own priesthood. Peter, you are in my prayers and my heart. Charlie Elmer

A month after receiving the email, I learned from the Apostolic Nuncio that I had been named Bishop of Little Rock. Somehow Charlie had heard the news in advance and had wanted to encourage me. Though puzzled by it that first month, I printed the email and have kept it in my breviary ever since.

It is, then, in devoted memory of Monsignor Charles W. Elmer's profound love for Christ and steadfast dedication to the priesthood (and in a sense at his direction) that I offer these words of encouragement to you, *my* sons and brothers in the Lord.

Ordination of Reverend Charles W. Elmer, December 20, 1952.

Introduction:
Strengthen Your Brothers

Dear Brothers in the Lord,

It struck me one evening not long after Pope Benedict XVI's 2008 visit to the United States that the words of Jesus to Simon are also his words to me as bishop and to you as brothers in the Lord. I began to consider writing a periodic message of encouragement to the priests of the Diocese of Joliet, and the idea seemed right. I pondered my own experiences as a priest, situations I have faced and face still, interior struggles in which I find myself engaged, moments of unexpected grace, lessons learned by the hardest, the joy that arises from loving and serving God's people, and the intimate link between priesthood and the cross. As I thought about all these things and more, I sensed the Lord saying to me: "Strengthen your brothers."

Thus from time to time I write simple and (I hope) helpful meditations on various aspects of our priestly lives—now for the priests of the Archdiocese of Seattle, but previously for those in the Diocese of Joliet. I keep a running list of potential topics, most unconnected to any particular occasion but simply reflections on situations we face, goals we strive to achieve, and graces God extends to us.

The context of the gospel verse on which I base the theme of these reflections is, of course, the Last Supper. In the course of the meal "an argument broke out among them about which of them should be regarded as the greatest." Jesus identified himself as the servant in their midst. Knowing that shortly Simon would turn away from him in denial, Jesus also knew that he would "turn back," and that, having turned back, he was to strengthen his brothers.

To personalize that context, let me say that the reflections I offer are from one who must "turn back" every day from his own denial, short-sightedness, selfishness, sin, and fear—to be strengthened by the Lord.

Luke is careful, and not in the least subtle, to remind us that the scene of Jesus' admonition to Simon and the others is the Last Supper. The Eucharist is the greatest source of priestly grace, strength, and encouragement—and ironically, by that very fact it is also the place where we confront our greatest need for mercy.

It is for that reason that my first encouragement to you, brothers in the Lord, is also the most important I will offer in this book: to celebrate Mass every day. The Eucharist is the essential environment in which we minister: from the Lord's table and his cross, to the midst of his people and all that our engagement with them entails, and back to his table and his cross. The efficacy of our day comes purely and entirely from his sacrifice. In fact, as I will suggest in another letter, priesthood is ministry *from the cross*.[1]

Father Paul Murray, OP, writes that when we receive the Body of the Lord, "we begin already, in some measure, to experience the joy of eternal life." Moreover, the phrase "Give us this day our daily bread" in the Lord's Prayer "contains in itself already an eternal day, even the promised day of resurrection." He quotes the *Catena Aurea of* St. Thomas Aquinas, in which is included a beautiful text from Pseudo-Augustine:

> It is not the [ordinary] bread which goes into our body, but the bread of everlasting life which gives support to the substance of our soul. . . . Take daily what profits you for the day, and so live that you may be worthy to receive. The death of the Lord is signified [by this bread], and the remission of sins. Whoever has a wound looks for medicine, and the wound is that we are under sin. The medicine is this heavenly and awesome sacrament. If you receive daily, daily does "Today" come to you. Christ is to you "Today." Christ rises to you daily.[2]

Poor, hungry men, we go to the altar every day to offer ourselves, to give thanks, and to be fed. Smiling, and with his hand on our shoulders, the Lord sends us to do his work—and accompanies us. He strengthens us that we might strengthen others.

It is my hope that these reflections speak to you of God's love and the beauty of our vocation in Christ, that they give you strength and hope, and that in a way uniquely suited to you, they help deepen your relationship with the Lord. May he be to us all the bread of "Today." May he rise in us "Today." And may he be, from the tips of our toes to the top of our heads and to the depth of our souls, our very "Today."

Sincerely in Christ,

+ *Peter Sartain*

Archbishop Peter Sartain

Notes

1. Letter 4, "Ministry From The Cross," pp. 23–26.

2. Paul Murray, OP, *Praying with Confidence: Aquinas on the Lord's Prayer* (London: Continuum, 2010), 70.

PRIESTLY IDENTITY IN CHRIST

1

With Boldness Unfettered

Dear Brothers in the Lord,

Get ready for a long journey. I'm about to take you from Memphis to Sheba to Seattle, and I hope you will bear with me.

After a visit to Memphis in 1988 at the invitation of then-Bishop Daniel Buechlein, Mother Teresa decided to open a shelter for homeless women and their children in the city. As chancellor for the diocese I was one of the point-persons for logistics, and in the process I got to know the regional superior of the Missionaries of Charity.

One day in late 1989, she called me. "Father, would you give two retreats to our sisters in North Yemen?" *North Yemen*? Incredulous, I told her I would consider the request but must ask the bishop's permission. With his nod, I said "yes" and started making arrangements for the trip the following March.

Someone suggested I call the American Embassy in Sana'a, the capital. Several years later, and much to my surprise, I came across the notes I had taken during that telephone conversation with a very helpful consul in Sana'a, Deborah.

At the top of the sheet I had written the date (1-20-90) and the embassy telephone number. Then, in short phrases, I had jotted down the following notes, based on Deborah's stern counsel:

> Bring minimum religious paraphernalia required. If asked religion, say, "Devout Christian." Occupation—not priest but something else.

On visa application, mark "visitor"—don't put "priest." No religious clothes. $150.00 to exchange immediately upon arrival. Cash better than traveler's checks. No credit cards. Altitude can exacerbate high blood pressure. Drink only bottled water and lots of it. Eat nothing fresh. Bring diarrhea medicine. *Conditions very primitive* [emphasis hers]. Few toilets. . . . Come to new embassy to register immediately upon arriving. Immunizations? *"Everything is rampant: meningitis, polio, typhus, typhoid, cholera, yellow fever, malaria, leprosy"* [again, emphasis hers].

On the day of my departure, I knew I was in for an adventure and took a deep breath. My mother worried. The bishop laughed.

Two days and multiple stops later, I arrived in Sana'a well after midnight. The sisters were there to greet me, and I spied their smiling faces through the fences as I nervously made my way through passport control and customs. As we drove through the deserted streets, I realized with deep apprehension that I was a visitor to another world, and the feeling only intensified as the moments went by. The sisters, completely at home in these surroundings but full of advice about what I should and should not do, took me to the house where I would be staying and left me alone. I went to bed.

When I awoke later that morning, I felt disoriented in a manner and to a degree I had never felt before: out-of-place, uneasy, alien, and alone. Since the sisters were to pick me up soon to celebrate Mass at the convent, I studied the Lectionary and began putting some thoughts together for the homily. The day's gospel reading was Matthew 12:38-42.

Then some of the scribes and Pharisees said to him, "Teacher, we wish to see a sign from you." He said to them in reply, "An evil and unfaithful generation seeks a sign, but no sign will be given it except the sign of Jonah the prophet. Just as Jonah was in the belly of the whale three days and three nights, so will the Son of Man be in the heart of the earth three days and three nights. At the judgment, the men of Nineveh will arise with this generation and condemn it, because they repented at the preaching of Jonah; and there is something greater than Jonah here. At the judgment the queen of the south will arise with this generation and condemn it, because she came from the ends of the earth to hear the wisdom of Solomon; and there is something greater than Solomon here."

The footnote in my Bible indicated, matter-of-factly: "The queen of the south came from Sheba, modern-day Yemen."

I shook my head in disbelief, smiled at the providential irony and thought: "Three thousand years ago, a wealthy queen from this very place travelled a world away to seek the unsurpassed wisdom of Solomon. And I am here with Wisdom from Someone greater than Solomon." This simple realization helped reorient me by giving me confidence in the Gospel I had come to preach. Truthfully, after I celebrated Mass for the sisters a few hours later, my anxiety diminished significantly.

I love the Book of Jonah, with its fantastic imagery and humor. Reading it, I think of southern Catholic writer Flannery O'Connor's outlandish—at times grotesque—exaggerations. As O'Connor saw it, she had a point to make, and only hyperbole would adequately express it. I think it was the same for the sacred author of Jonah. The reluctant prophet had run from God's call because he judged the mission to be quixotic, even ludicrous: "Preach conversion to the *Ninevites?* God must be kidding or out of his mind," he reasoned. God had the last laugh, of course, because when Jonah did eventually take up his mission and preach, "Forty days more and Nineveh shall be destroyed," it took merely a day for the Ninevites to believe God. The king decreed a kingdom-wide fast of repentance for human and animal alike, hoping that God would "relent and forgive, and withhold his blazing wrath, so that we might not perish." Seeing the people's repentance, God did not carry out the destruction he had sent Jonah to proclaim as a warning. Incredibly, Jonah was miffed at what he saw as God's reckless display of mercy. Who, then, was in greater need of conversion: the Ninevites or Jonah? God had more lessons to teach him, and chief among them was this—do not confuse your reluctance to preach God's Word with the people's readiness to receive it.

Jesus used the stories of the Queen of Sheba and Jonah to expose the unadulterated stubbornness of the scribes and Pharisees. He reminded them that even notorious pagans had once sought and listened to Solomon's wisdom and repented at Jonah's reluctant preaching. Why were these scribes and Pharisees so trapped in their disbelief, so stubborn in their blind refusal to see that he was greater than Solomon? The inescapable truth they refused to face was the true identity of Jesus, the unadulterated truth of his teaching. Even the Queen of Sheba and the Ninevites would have caught on.

It was when I reflected on the speed with which the Ninevites accepted Jonah's preaching that I remembered that morning in Sana'a in 1990. Jesus had brought the two images together to teach that we can have complete confidence in God's power at work in the preaching of the

Gospel. There's a bit of Jonah's reluctance in every preacher of the Word: "What if they reject this extraordinary message, this challenging teaching, this preacher himself?" When we allow the fear of rejection to shake our confidence or dilute the Word, God says: "Don't forget the Ninevites. Don't forget the Queen of Sheba. Don't forget the determination of my Son, who placed total confidence in me. Trust the Word and preach it with confidence and boldness, love and humility, despite your fear and hesitation."

I love this excerpt—at once fiery and touching—from the writings of St. Francis of Assisi. After sharply instructing his readers about the menace of evil and the need to repent, he takes a tender turn.

> In the love which is God we beg all those whom these words reach to receive those fragrant words of our Lord Jesus Christ written above with divine love and kindness. *And let whoever does not know how to read have them read to them frequently* [emphasis mine]. Because they are spirit and life, they should preserve them together with a holy activity to the end.[1]

Francis had complete confidence in the Word. He himself had been converted by it, and he knew that its words of spirit and life must be preached boldly, confidently, lovingly, and constantly for the sake of all—even read, frequently, to those who cannot read. It is an act of tender love to read to another. Don't parents read lovingly to their little ones, even read the same favorite story over and over? The Word will do its work, but it must be proclaimed, even when we ourselves are skeptical of its demands and implausible hope.

It seems to me that among the characteristics called for by the New Evangelization, the most important are delight, awe, wonder, adoration, confidence, boldness, humility, and love. These are the very qualities that marked the preaching of Sts. Peter and Paul.

Several years ago, while visiting the Capitoline Museum in Rome, I discovered Pompeo Batoni's *Holy Family*. At that time the painting was hanging in a grand staircase, and as I ascended the stairs I was immediately captivated by the magnificent expression on Joseph's face. The word I think best describes his expression is *delight*. Joseph is full of delight as he looks at Jesus and Mary. They are the major figures in the painting, but Joseph's facial expression captures an important element for all preaching and teaching: loving delight in the mystery of salvation in Christ Jesus.

Pompeo Batoni, *The Holy Family*, c. 1760. Oil on canvas, 99 x 74 cm. The Capitoline Museums, Rome.

Paul was constantly in awe that he, a former persecutor and "the very least of all the holy ones," had been given a special grace "for your benefit," a revelation and insight into the mystery of Christ, a grace "to preach to the Gentiles the inscrutable riches of Christ, and to bring to light [for all] what is the plan of the mystery hidden from ages past in God who created all things (Eph 3:1-9). So overpowering was this grace that he would write, "Woe to me if I do not preach the [gospel]!" (1 Cor 9:16). But even as he delighted in this unexpected grace and reflected on the fact that he had no choice but to do what God asked of him, he realized how far he had to go personally ("Miserable one that I am!" Rom 7:24).

We priests of the Word must ourselves be so captivated by the mystery of faith that our delight in the mystery shines with infectious joy in all we do. Delight is evidenced in wonder, awe, enthusiasm, and love. It is seasoned with the humble acknowledgment that we are sinners, works in progress. It is fed and grows in silent contemplation, prayer, and adoration. It is wonder that literally never ceases.

And, as St. Paul knew well, because it is above all the recognition that with God everything is grace, delight gives birth to confidence and boldness. According to the New Testament, such confident boldness is the gift of the Spirit.

Paul decides to write boldly to the Christians at Rome precisely because God had *graced* him with the office of Apostle to the Gentiles. In fact, he understands his ministry as that of a priest in service to the Messiah, preparing the Gentiles as a worthy offering to God. In his priestly service, slaughtered animals would be replaced by a repentant people. Moreover, he finds full confidence in the new covenant. Whereas Moses veiled his face and the glory shining on it—"its glory that was going to fade"—Paul writes that "since we have such hope, we act very boldly and not like Moses," because "whenever a person turns to the Lord the veil is removed" (2 Cor 3:11-16). "All of us, gazing with unveiled face on the glory of the Lord, are being transformed into the same image from glory to glory, as from the Lord who is the Spirit" (2 Cor 3:18). He is amazed, in awe, in adoration, delighted—and *very* bold. God's grace, the blood of a new covenant in Christ Jesus, and the Holy Spirit make him so.

After healing a crippled beggar "in the name of Jesus Christ the Nazorean," Peter began teaching the gathering crowd, upsetting the priests, temple guard, and Sadducees. Peter and John were taken into custody until the next day, when they were brought into the presence of leaders, elders, scribes, and high priests for interrogation. By what power or by what name had they accomplished this healing? Peter, "filled with the holy Spirit," answered them with such confidence that "Observing the boldness of Peter and John and perceiving them to be uneducated, ordinary men, they were amazed, and they recognized them as companions of Jesus" (Acts 4:13).

Realizing that Peter and John would not and could not stop speaking "about what we have seen and heard," the leaders released them with a warning.

> After their release they went back to their own people and reported what the chief priests and elders had told them. And when they heard it, they raised their voices to God with one accord: . . . "And now, Lord, take note of their threats, and enable your servants to speak your word with all boldness, as you stretch forth [your] hand to heal, and signs and wonders are done through the name of your holy servant Jesus." As they prayed, the place where they were gathered shook, and they were all filled with the holy Spirit and continued to speak the word of God with boldness. (Acts 4:20-31)

The Acts of the Apostles and virtually all New Testament letters refer to this same boldness and confidence which are the work of the Holy

Spirit through faith in Christ. This gift of the Spirit—this Truth who is Christ—this power from Christ's death and resurrection—empower the apostles to continue preaching despite every opposition and personal fear. Because it is literally God's work for which they are mere servants, they can do their part confidently and leave the results (mysterious in themselves) to God.

> Therefore, since we have this ministry through the mercy shown us, we are not discouraged. . . . For we do not preach ourselves but Jesus Christ as Lord, and ourselves as your slaves for the sake of Jesus. For God who said, "Let light shine out in darkness," has shone in our hearts to bring to light the knowledge of the glory of God in the face of [Jesus] Christ.

> But we hold this treasure in earthen vessels, that the surpassing power may be of God and not from us. We are afflicted in every way, but not constrained; perplexed but not driven to despair; persecuted, but not abandoned; struck down, but not destroyed; always carrying about in the body the dying of Jesus, so that the life of Jesus may also be manifested in our body. . . .

> So death is at work in us, but life in you. Since, then, we have the same spirit of faith, according to what is written, "I believed, therefore I spoke," we too believe and therefore we speak, knowing that the one who raised the Lord Jesus will raise us also with Jesus and place us with you in his presence. . . .

> Therefore, we are not discouraged. (2 Cor 4:1-16)

There is one attitude that must never appear in any effort of the New Evangelization: *arrogance*. Arrogance is a counter-sign to the Gospel and justly repels those who truly thirst for God. With Paul, "we do not preach ourselves but Jesus Christ as Lord." "I will not dare to speak of anything except what Christ has accomplished through me" (Rom 15:18). The arrogant preacher preaches not Christ but himself. Run from arrogance.

Another reason for confidence, according to St. Paul, is that God is at work in those who thirst for and listen to his Word. "I am confident of this, that the one who began a good work in you will continue to complete it until the day of Christ Jesus" (Phil 1:6). "We are confident of you in the Lord that what we instruct you, you [both] are doing and will continue to do" (2 Thess 3:4). "I myself am convinced about you, my brothers, that you yourselves are full of goodness" (Rom 15:14).

Amid this talk of confidence and boldness, it is important to reflect on an intriguing and inescapable aspect of the call to teach and preach the Word: the mystery of rejection. Blessed John Paul II once wrote that after some initial success preaching to the Athenians, who were fascinated with his reference to "an unknown God," Paul evoked their fearsome protest when he mentioned the resurrection. But he was not deterred.

> The apostle then understood that the mystery of salvation in Christ would not be easily accepted by the Greeks, accustomed as they were to mythology and to various forms of philosophical specula-tion. Nevertheless, he did not lay down his weapons. After his set-back at Athens, he nonetheless continued with *holy stubbornness* to proclaim the Gospel to every creature. This holy stubbornness finally led him to Rome, where he met his death.[2]

Why does God permit some to reject his Word, to reject the gift of faith? If the message is for all, why will some never hear it? This mystery re-flects God's respect for human freedom, his patience, and the deeper, hidden working of his grace. When we see him face-to-face, then we will understand. Until then, he gives the Church holy stubbornness to persevere.

There is indeed a bit of Jonah's reluctance in all of us. We can be tempted to timidity when preaching the Word, fearing rejection or wondering if the scandals that have rocked the Church in recent years have destroyed our credibility or the credibility of the Word itself. Will people even listen? We might ask rhetorically whether it is too late to preach the Word in our secular culture, whether people have moved definitively and permanently away from the things of God.

But we preach not ourselves but Jesus, the Word of the Father, who sends the Holy Spirit not only to us who preach but also to those who hear.

I have long been fascinated by the way Luke ends the Acts of the Apostles. Having preached and healed in the name of Jesus with much success and much rejection, having found himself literally in chains for having done what the Lord sent him to do, having survived shipwreck and the mean-spirited manipulation of those who actively worked against the Word of God, having escaped the deadly threat of a viper clinging to his hand, Paul finds himself in Rome under benign house arrest, allowed to preach in peace to those who come to him. Here he was, in the capital of the ancient world, and Luke thus reminds us that the Word had spread to "the ends of the earth." But the end of Acts is in fact open-ended: "He remained for two full years in his lodgings. He received all who came to him, and with complete assurance and without hindrance he proclaimed the kingdom of God and taught about the Lord Jesus Christ" (28:30-31).

Some have suggested that the final verse could be appropriately translated: "he proclaimed the kingdom of God and taught about the Lord Jesus Christ *with boldness unfettered.*"

My brothers in the Lord, as God unfolds for us his desires for the New Evangelization, my prayer is that both as individual priests and as a presbyterate we will grow in our delight in the mystery of faith, our trust in the Gospel who is Christ Jesus, our humble confidence and boldness in preaching the Word in this very secular culture, our love for every person in this part of the Lord's vineyard, our spirit of sacrifice which flows from and back to the Eucharist, and our prayerful adoration of the One who loves us with infinite love.

And may we never forget that as we preach the powerful and challenging Word of God in this place, the likes of the wealthy Queen of Sheba, the fearsome Ninevites, the fanatical Saul, and the youthful Francesco Bernardone are listening—thirsting—for the Truth we bear in earthen vessels. Remember what God can do with a mustard seed, a little yeast, a grain of wheat. Some will reject him, but think what will happen in those who receive him. May we live and preach the Word with boldness unfettered. God's Word will do his work.

I can offer no better advice to end this letter than that which St. Catherine of Siena offered to her close friend, Fra Bartolomeo Dominici:

> And so set yourself
> to do everything bravely,
> and drive out darkness
> and establish light
> without considering
> your weakness.
> But believe that
> through Christ Crucified
> you can do everything.[3]

Sincerely in Christ,

+ *Peter Sartain*

Archbishop Peter Sartain

P.S. Two months after I returned home a few pounds lighter, North Yemen reunited with South Yemen, healing a breach that had existed since the nineteenth century. A priest friend in Memphis sent me a note of congratulations, crediting me with the feat. I thanked him. The Yemeni visa stamped in my passport aroused suspicion at every port of entry for several years until that passport expired.

Notes

1. Saint Francis of Assisi, "Earlier Exhortation," in *Francis of Assisi: Early Documents,* vol. 1, ed. Regis J. Armstrong, J.A. Wayne Hellman, and William J. Short (Hyde Park, NY: New City Press, 1999), 44.

2. His Holiness John Paul II, *Crossing the Threshold of Hope* (New York: Alfred A. Knopf, 1994), 106–7.

3. Saint Catherine of Siena, Letter T200, author's translation.

2

Responding to God's Call

Dear Brothers in the Lord,

Perhaps you feel at times as I do—astounded that the Lord would choose me for his extraordinary work. And yet he has chosen us all.

This thought brings to mind Henry Ossawa Tanner's painting of *The Annunciation*, located in the Philadelphia Museum of Art.

Born in 1859, Tanner was reared the son of a minister in an affluent African-American family. He began his art career in 1876, taking him from his childhood home of Philadelphia to Atlanta, Paris, the Holy Land, and back to the United States. His work came to be celebrated worldwide, but especially in France, where the French government honored him with several national awards.

I came across Tanner's *The Annunciation* several years ago when I visited a bishop-friend who was ill. A framed copy of the painting hung in his chapel, and it captivated me immediately.

What caught me was the peaceful, attentive expression on the young Mary's face and the depiction of an ordinary, unadorned room, complete with rumpled sheets and nightclothes. Even the light suggesting the presence of the angel is subtle and peace-filled, as if this apparition, though astounding and surprising, was intended not to frighten but to fulfill. It could have been anyone's bedroom, and yet it was Mary's. It could have been any young woman, and yet it was Mary. It was Mary's Moment—the moment that would define her response to the extraordinary grace she had already received.

Henry Ossawa Tanner, *The Annunciation*, 1898. Oil on canvas, 57 x 71.25 in. Philadelphia Museum of Art.

The Office of Readings for December 20 includes these words from a homily "In Praise of the Virgin Mother" by St. Bernard of Clairvaux:

> You have heard, O Virgin, that you will conceive and bear a son; you have heard that it will not be by man but by the Holy Spirit. The angel awaits an answer; it is time for him to return to God who sent him. We too are waiting, O Lady, for your word of compassion. . . .
>
> Tearful Adam with his sorrowing family begs this of you, O loving Virgin, in their exile from Paradise. Abraham begs it, David begs it. All the other holy patriarchs, your ancestors, ask it of you, as they dwell in the country of the shadow of death. This is what the whole earth waits for, prostrate at your feet. It is right in doing so, for on your word depends comfort for the wretched, ransom for the captive, freedom for the condemned, indeed, salvation for all the sons of Adam, the whole of your race.
>
> Answer quickly, O Virgin. . . . Answer with a word, receive the Word of God. Speak your own word, conceive the divine Word. Breathe a passing word, embrace the eternal Word.

Tanner's painting and Bernard's sermon make me reflect on something that often rolls around in my heart: God calls me to cooperate trustingly with his plan, even though the full lines of that plan remain a complete and utter mystery to me and even though he often leaves me shaking my head in wonder. In recent years, I have come to realize in a new way that God asks that I allow myself to be "moved" both figuratively and literally by his will, that I learn to float easily on the tides of his providence, and that I cast objections and second-guessing aside and simply say: "Yes." I hope and pray that the lesson will sink in deeply and thoroughly.

I have also been pondering my response to invitations from God to place myself at his disposal in the seemingly routine events of every day. Situations I have faced thousands of times before—passing a stranger on the street, attending a meeting, returning a phone call, preparing a homily, visiting the hospital—might be the moment for which the person before me has been waiting, the moment God will use to make himself known to him or her.

Am I willing to place myself at God's disposal in those moments as well as the larger Moments? Will I trust that they also are part of the unfolding of his plan and that he asks me to consciously cooperate as generously as I can?

God has used the books of Fr. Walter Ciszek, SJ, to pose these important questions to me. *With God in Russia* and *He Leadeth Me* chronicle the twenty-three years Ciszek spent in Soviet prisons and Siberian labor camps after being arrested and convicted of being a Vatican spy during World War II.[1]

Reading the first book I was constantly amazed at his strength in the face of the distressing conditions in which he lived those twenty-three years. I found myself asking again and again, "How did he do it? Could *I* do it?" The second book unfolds his simple and persuasive secrets: daily Mass; committed prayer; and the fact that each day, to each person and in each circumstance, one moment at a time, he handed himself over to God to be used as God wished. He did this because he saw the circumstances of each day as God's will for him.

> To predict what God's will is going to be, to rationalize about what his will must be, is at once a work of human folly and yet the subtlest of all temptations. The plain and simple truth is that his will is what he actually wills to send us each day, in the way of circumstances, places, people, and problems. The trick is to learn to see that—not just in theory, or not just occasionally in a flash of insight granted by God's grace, but every day. Each of us has no need to wonder about what God's will must be for us; his will for us is clearly re-

vealed in every situation of every day, if only we could learn to view all things as he sees them and sends them to us.[2]

. . .

What he wanted was for me to accept these situations as from his hands, to let go of the reins and place myself entirely at his disposal. He was asking of me an act of total trust, allowing for no interference or restless striving on my part, no reservations, no exceptions, no areas where I could set conditions or seem to hesitate. He was asking a complete gift of self, nothing held back. It demanded absolute faith: faith in God's existence, in his providence, in his concern for the minutest detail, in his power to sustain me, and in his love protecting me. It meant losing the last hidden doubt, the ultimate fear that God will not be there to bear you up.[3]

Mary's Moment, and her response, changed everything; they became the paradigm for a disciple's every moment, a disciple's every response. In the stuff of today's appointments, the rumpled chaos of our rooms and offices, in the chance meetings that punctuate the day, in our celebration of Mass and our times of prayer, in the irritating and the unexplainable, in the painful and the peaceful, we encounter God's will—our moment and opportunity to respond. To borrow Bernard's image, who might be awaiting our response to God's invitation to cooperate with his plan today?

Sincerely in Christ,

+ Peter Sartain

Archbishop Peter Sartain

Notes

1. Walter J. Ciszek, SJ, with Daniel L. Flaherty, SJ, *With God in Russia* (San Francisco: Ignatius Press, 1997) and *He Leadeth Me* (San Francisco: Ignatius Press, 1995).

2. Ibid., p. 39.

3. Ibid., p. 77.

3

The Priest as Father

Dear Brothers in the Lord,

Perhaps you've seen the 1987 movie by French writer-director Louis Malle, *Au revoir, les enfants* (Goodbye, children). Based on events from Malle's childhood, the film tells the true story of Julien Quentin, a twelve-year-old student at an elite prep school run by Discalced Carmelite friars near Paris during World War II. Defying German anti-Semitic policies, the friars secretly enroll three Jewish boys under assumed names. One of the boys, Jean Bonnet, is assigned as Julien's roommate. Their relationship begins in rivalry, but they eventually become close friends who share a solemn secret. When the Gestapo learns the truth, Jean, the other two Jewish boys, and the school's priest-headmaster are arrested. Although the headmaster's role in the film is small, his final farewell to the children gives the film its title.

There was much more to his story. Lucien-Louis Bunel was born in 1900 to a devout working-class family and held a lifelong commitment to prayer and social justice. Ordained a diocesan priest in 1925, he entered the Discalced Carmelites in 1931 and was given the name "Jacques de Jesus." He was appointed headmaster of the prep school, but the assignment was interrupted by a compulsory stint in the French military. As chaplain to troops along the Maginot Line, he published a simple newsletter with words of encouragement for his men. One of the important topics he wanted to address was fatherhood.

> Let us talk a little bit about . . . your children, shall we? You see,
> after the age of eight or ten, without any notice, your son will spy
> on you. One day or another he will have heard some of his friends,
> who have lost all respect for their fathers, mock them by exposing
> their lies, by making fun of their orders, and by perhaps revealing
> the seamy side of their private lives. Your son, back home, will
> silently keep an eye on you. He will listen to you talk, he will inves-
> tigate your life with an amazing, childlike anguish, until he is able
> to form an opinion. Then one day he will throw himself into your
> arms effusively, with tears maybe, covering you with caresses. You
> will not understand, but he will have learned with a delirious joy
> and exciting pride that you are not like the father of his friend, that
> you did not lie, that you, his father, were honest, decent, and pure.
> Your son will then be so completely proud of you![1]

After military service, he took up the headmaster's role again, now in
an occupied France. It was then that he enrolled the three Jewish boys,
fully aware that if discovered he could lose his life. The boys were shel-
tered, loved, and educated just like the other students, but once exposed
they were arrested along with Père Jacques. The boys were immediately
deported to Auschwitz where they were executed, and Père Jacques was
imprisoned in a concentration camp at Mauthausen, where its rigors and
filth wreaked havoc on his health. Liberated by American troops in May
1945, he died less than a month later. His selfless ministry in the camps
became legendary, and both the State of Israel and the United States
Holocaust Memorial Museum have honored him as a rescuer—one of
the "Righteous Among the Nations."

As priest Jacques Bunel was a father, too, and he took his fatherhood
seriously. He had told his troops,

> The war has torn you away from your home, from your wife, and
> from your children. More than once in the corner of a field or a barn
> I have surprised you, as you were thinking of them with emotion
> and with pain. Because of my priestly celibacy, I will always be
> without children. I wish you could know how I would have loved
> my children. I truly understand your pain, your deep pain, born of
> this temporary separation.[2]

So would we have understood. When we committed our lives to celibacy, we made a complete gift of ourselves—a sacrifice—to the Lord and
the Church, as a husband to his wife. We said: "I am yours." It is from

that gift of ourselves that our spiritual fatherhood arises, and one of the graces of celibacy is that in Christ our family expands to include those to whom he sends us. No matter their age, race, culture, or language, they are our children—and they have a claim on us.

> The disciples were amazed at his words. So Jesus again said to them in reply, "Children, how hard it is to enter the kingdom of God!" . . . Peter began to say to him, "We have given up everything and followed you." Jesus said, "Amen, I say to you, there is no one who has given up house or brothers or sisters or mother or father or children or lands for my sake and for the sake of the gospel who will not receive a hundred times more now in this present age: houses and brothers and sisters and mothers and children and lands, with persecutions, and eternal life in the age to come." (Mark 10:24-31)

Having heard Jesus speak about the demands of the reign of God, Peter wondered how he could expect more than they had already pledged: "We have given up everything!" Focused on himself and the deprivations the reign of God seemed to demand, Peter asked if it could get any harder. Jesus, speaking to the disciples as his "children," directed their attention not to the deprivation of giving all for the kingdom but to the gift of universal fatherhood—and the gift of the cross.

Taking the part of Jesus in the reading of the passion, I am always struck by his determination, his courage, his humility, and most especially his love for the flock. Without such love, how could he have endured the passion and all it entailed? From God's perspective, we are the pearl of great price, the buried treasure, the lost coin, the lost sheep, the lost son, the unforgiving ones with the unpayable debt. We must mean much more to him than we imagine, that he would give his Son for us, stingy as we are with our love and fickle in our faithfulness.

I have another experience whenever the passion is proclaimed. I keep finding myself taking the part of the crowd, too, because I realize that I am one of those for whom he paid the ransom. I am one of the ungrateful ones, one of those whose flesh tires and fails to keep watch with him. I speak the words of Jesus—called by him to be his priest and love his flock—but I am as indebted to him as anyone else, and probably more.

As Holy Week unfolds, we will continue to take the part of Jesus and in doing so will be reminded who we are. On Thursday we will wash our parishioners' feet, for in Jesus we are to be their never-failing servants. On Friday when we walk into our churches, the first thing we will do is prostrate ourselves on the floor—just as we did at ordination—to show our emptiness before God, to submit ourselves to him without condition, to ask that he fill us with himself. We will then be the first to kiss the cross, because shepherds should give example to the flock.

The General Instruction of the Roman Missal suggests that the priest take off his shoes when venerating the cross on Good Friday. As I take off my shoes, my first thought is about the humility symbolized by this peculiar public act; but when I walk toward the cross in sock-feet, my experience quickly changes into one of vulnerability. I feel strangely unsteady and embarrassed to make a gesture that proclaims the centrality of the cross in my life as priest. Do my actions the other days of the year proclaim the same thing, or is this an empty ritual act?

Saint Gregory Nazianzen suggests that we picture ourselves in various roles in the passion. He adds:

> So let us take our part in the Passover prescribed by the law, not in a literal way, but according to the teaching of the Gospel; not in an imperfect way, but perfectly; not only for a time, but eternally . . . I will say more: we must sacrifice ourselves to God, each day and in everything we do, accepting all that happens to us for the sake of the Word, imitating his passion by our sufferings, and honoring his blood by shedding our own. We must be ready to be crucified.[3]

It is of the nature of fatherhood that, having been instrumental in the creation of life, the father is willing to lay down his life for his children. The same is true for us who are fathers in faith, who nurture a spiritual family under God's reign.

Saint Paul understood his relationship to the churches as father to children.

> With such affection for you, we were determined to share with you not only the gospel of God, but our very selves as well, so dearly beloved had you become to us. . . . As you know, we treated each one of you as a father treats his children, exhorting and encouraging you and insisting that you conduct yourselves as worthy of the God who calls you into his kingdom and glory. (1 Thess 2:8, 11-12)

I cannot help but call to mind Paul's letter to Philemon. Philemon's slave, Onesimus (Useful), had run away; during his absence he was befriended and converted by Paul, who sent him back to his owner with these words:

> I rather urge you out of love, being as I am, Paul, an old man, and
> now also a prisoner for Christ Jesus. I urge you on behalf of my child
> Onesimus, whose father I have become in my imprisonment, who
> was once useless to you but is now useful to [both] you and me. I am
> sending him, that is, my own heart, back to you. . . . Perhaps this
> is why he was away from you for a while, that you might have him
> back forever, no longer as a slave but more than a slave, a brother,
> beloved especially to me, but even more so to you, as a man and in
> the Lord. (Phlm 9-12, 15-16)

The context of Paul's words is not priestly ministry, but the underlying
meaning fits our context. Paul's relationship with Onesimus was that of
father in faith, and it had changed everything for him, for Onesimus,
and—Paul hoped—for Philemon. They were all "in the Lord."

The fact that our parishioners refer to us as "Father" is a daily reminder
of our relationship to them in the Lord. At this time when so many families are bereft of fathers, our role is particularly important. We are fathers
to young and old. I fondly recall kids playing in the gyms, fields, and
parking lots of my parishes, for whom I was "Fr. Pete." But just as fondly
I recall a seventy-year-old man in my office who burst into bitter tears
when he recounted how his father had mistreated him. He came to his
spiritual father for comfort and healing.

> To give life—the graced life of the sacraments.
> To pour ourselves out—as a sacrifice.
> To guide, nurture, and comfort—with loving, attentive presence.
> To form God's family as sisters and brothers—in spiritual fatherhood.

Our role as fathers is to sustain the family that is our parish and to
love our parishioners as we would our own children. Would I give my
life for them? Do I?

Father Jacques Bunel was more than headmaster to the students. He
was their father. As the children bade him farewell the day he was arrested, their cautious words grew louder by the moment: *"Au revoir, mon
Père!"* He turned to them, waved, and said: *"Au revoir, les enfants."*

As I take the part of Jesus in the passion and realize all it required of
him, I ask myself: "How could he do it?" I hear him respond: "How
could I not?"

My brothers in the Lord, may the Sacred Triduum and our celebration
of the Easter season deepen our awareness of God's love. Deep down,

in the secret of our hearts, may we give ourselves anew to him and to our children. I am your father, and you have my prayers every day.

Sincerely in Christ,

+ *Peter Sartain*

Archbishop Peter Sartain

Notes

1. Francis J. Murphy, *Père Jacques: Resplendent in Victory* (Washington, DC: ICS Publications, 1998), 144–45.

2. Ibid., 143–44.

3. Gregory of Nazianzen, *Oratio* 45, 23–24.

4

Ministry from the Cross

Dear Brothers in the Lord,

"James" Joseph-Jacques Tissot was born at Nantes, France, in 1836. After studying at the Academy of Fine Arts in Paris, he began a celebrated career as a painter and illustrator. While working on a painting about a woman singing in church, he regularly attended liturgy, and it was there that he found inspiration for another painting, *Christ the Comforter* (ca. 1884, The Hermitage Museum, St. Petersburg). This painting marked the beginning of a new stage in his art and, ultimately, a new stage in his life. So attracted was he to the figure of Christ that he made several trips to the Holy Land, and then spent ten years painting a series of watercolors, which he eventually published as *The Life of Our Lord Jesus Christ*—365 drawings of gospel themes and accompanying notes. The original watercolors can be found in the Brooklyn Museum.[1]

I had never heard of Tissot until I made a retreat in Assisi, the birthplace of St. Francis, to mark my twenty-fifth anniversary of ordination to the priesthood. Walking Assisi's hilly, cobbled streets, I passed a small, half-empty shop selling antique drawings and prints. Eyeing several religious prints in a window display, I decided to go inside. After browsing a few minutes, I came across an old colored lithograph titled *What Our Saviour Saw from the Cross*, by J. J. Tissot. Hoping that I would buy the print, the shopkeeper assured me that Tissot was famous.

James J. Tissot, *What Our Lord Saw from the Cross*, c. 1890. Watercolor over graphite on wove paper, 24.8 x 23 cm. Brooklyn Museum.

I was immediately drawn not just to the drawing, but especially to its theme. It is a downward view of a crowd from the cross, through the eyes of Jesus. The viewer stares directly into the eyes of Mary and other grieving women, and the scene is filled with a motley assembly of characters: a Roman soldier standing defiantly at guard; shepherds squatting with staffs in hand; three men (kings?) on luxuriously saddled horses; official-looking elders off-handedly observing from the rear; simple people, men and women, caught up in the somber events; casual passersby gawking out of curiosity.

Jesus is, in fact, the focal point. But Tissot makes the viewers the focal point as well, because the crowd seems to be staring at us. What emerges is a kind of identification of the viewers with Jesus: he gazes from the cross at those for whom he gave his life, and we see them through his eyes.

What I like most about the painting is what it taught me: that priestly ministry is ministry *from the cross*. If we serve *in persona Christi*, that means we are not just envoys with a message, not just deliverers of the fruit, but ministers in him *from the cross*. Our people look to us as to Christ, and they have a right to. And from the cross, however the Lord has asked us to bear it with him, we gaze upon them in a loving, self-offering embrace. We are *for you*, we might say, because we are *in him*.

Even more, our priestly vocation flows from the cross and leads to the cross. A life of holiness gazes upon the cross in prayer. The life of priestly ministry entails loving from the cross in one unfolding act of self-oblation. That is why the Eucharist will always stand at the center of our ministry and at the center of the life of the Church; it is also why intercessory prayer before the Blessed Sacrament is an important part of the ministry of priests.

Because a priest's ministry must never be reduced to mere administration, the bishops gathered for the Tenth Ordinary General Assembly of the Synod of Bishops focused on what the episcopate entails for the personal life of the bishop and for the exercise of the ministry entrusted to him. In the post-synodal document, *Pastores Gregis*, Blessed John Paul II writes:

> The ontological transformation brought about by episcopal consecration, as a configuration to Christ, demands a lifestyle that manifests a "being with him." Consequently, during the Synod sessions, emphasis was laid on pastoral charity as being the fruit of the character bestowed by the sacrament and of its particular grace. Charity, it was said, is in a sense the heart of the ministry of the Bishop, who is drawn into a dynamic pastoral *pro-existence* whereby he is impelled to live, like Christ the Good Shepherd, for the Father and for others, in the daily gift of self. (11)
>
> Here it is not only a matter of an *existentia* but indeed of a *pro-existentia*, that is to say, of a way of living inspired by the supreme model of Christ the Lord and which is spent totally in worship of the Father and in service of neighbor. (13)

What Blessed John Paul wrote about the ministry of bishops is equally instructive for all priests. Our ministry is *for others* precisely because we have been made and ordained *for the worship of God*. Saying "yes" to the cross means not only that we give ourselves to God—for with Jesus, from the cross, we priests are also *given* by the Father to those he loves. Having *given ourselves to him,* and *having been given by him* to shepherd those he loves, we belong to all, and they to us.

Sincerely in Christ,

+ *Peter Sartain*

Archbishop Peter Sartain

Note

1. The collection has been reissued in book form by the Brooklyn Museum as *James Tissot: The Life of Christ,* ed. Judith F. Dolkart (London: Merrell, 2009).

5

Kissing the Altar

Dear Brothers in the Lord,

Will we kiss the altar every day?

After celebrating Mass for a large group of teenagers, I joined them at a restaurant and visited each table, joking as I went along. In a rare moment of seriousness, a seventeen-year-old boy admitted in front of his friends, "Bishop, during your homily I almost teared up inside." After several seconds of silence, those sitting at his table erupted in laughter, chiding him for "almost" tearing up "inside."

I knew what he meant, as they did, but we couldn't resist laughing. When I was a young man, I teared up inside but rarely outside. As I have gotten older, the tears flow more freely and more frequently. They flow when I hear a favorite song sung well, at the death of a loved one, at a joyous occasion celebrated with friends, or during an emotional scene in a movie (one of the closing scenes in *Field of Dreams* gets me every time).

There are also moments in the liturgy that catch me off guard because of their intensity and cause my eyes to water: ordinations and the Mass of Chrism particularly come to mind. One of my favorite liturgies is the dedication of a church because of the care given to the anointing of the altar. I often find myself welling up with tears as I spread chrism across the mensa with my right hand.

When we pass through our parish churches, we bow to the altar at which we offer Mass, in an act of reverence for Christ. Hebrews presents him as the high priest and living altar of the heavenly temple, and the

Fathers suggested that he was the victim, priest, and altar of his own sacrifice. The altar is a sacred sign, whether it is made of stone or wood, or whether it stands in the cathedral or in a tiny rural parish. Its meaning is so powerful that no one should ever pass an altar without bowing to Christ present there.

But the priest also kisses the altar. This is a very public gesture made in the presence of those gathered for the Eucharist; but it is at the same time an intensely private gesture, an act of affection and surrender, an act of love and trust. Even more to the point, the priest's kiss of the altar is an act of identification: he is proclaiming to Christ, to himself, and to his parishioners that it is Christ the Priest who makes him who he is. We kiss the altar that is a sign of the Lord himself, the sacrifice of Calvary, and the table of the Last Supper. Everything we do flows from the altar and back to it. The kiss symbolizes our daily embrace of the sacrifice of Christ as our way of life, for on the day of our ordination we were totally and irrevocably joined in character to him.

Some days it's easy to kiss the altar. At our first Masses, we knew the sheer joy of experiencing the outpouring of the Holy Spirit at the hands of the bishop, the wonder at God's goodness in calling us to the priesthood. Who would not kiss the altar in gratitude for such undeserved blessing?

Again and again we kiss the altar at celebrations of daily Mass, at weddings and anniversaries, at ordinations and other gatherings of the Church. We stand behind the altar not because we are better than others but because we bear the identity of Christ, the only true priest, who came not to be served but to serve and to *give himself* in sacrifice.

There are also sad occasions when we priests kiss the altar, as we lead God's people in prayer with Christ the Consoler, the One who knows our pain and the grief of death, the One who announced "Peace!" when he found his apostles gathered in fear after his resurrection from the dead. Then we stand with Christ the Giver of Hope, who in times of difficulty trusted wholeheartedly in the providence of his Father.

Sometimes when we kiss the altar only we know the nature of the cross we bear. Perhaps we are keenly pained by the weight of our sinfulness, so our kiss symbolizes our need for Christ's mercy. Perhaps at other times our kiss is a deliberate act of the will and a prayer that he will help us understand the very personal challenges we are facing. Perhaps at times it is a simple act of love: "I love you, Christ, my Lord."

In every circumstance, we priests kiss the altar as a dramatic reminder of who we are and who we are called to follow, and as a proclamation to our parishioners that everything about us is *for them*. The gesture has become so important to me that I begin and end my holy hour by kissing the altar. Doing so reminds me that as a priest I both pray and minister *from the cross.*

Jesus forever set the standard for sacrifice by giving himself, not something to represent himself. He did so willingly, whole-heartedly, completely, to let the Father's power be known.

"This is why the Father loves me, because I lay down my life in order to take it up again. No one takes it from me, but I lay it down on my own" (John 10:17-18).

Just as Jesus held nothing back from his Father, neither did the saints who followed him, nor do the saints we know in our parishes. Their wholehearted gift of self was accepted and transformed by God. They discovered that they were refreshed, revitalized, and even given the strength to do what they thought they could never do. They surrendered their all, and their emptiness was filled with God's All. I often look to the saints for inspiration when I find that I am letting my all be wrenched from me rather than giving it freely: "whoever loses his life for my sake will find it" (Matt 10:39).

It is quite possible that some day our all will be taken from us by illness, tragedy, or even by assignment in a way we never anticipated. During a symposium in 1995 marking the thirtieth anniversary of the Decree on the Ministry and Life of Priests (*Presbyterorum ordinis*), Cardinal Miloslav Vlk of Prague said that in order to survive and thrive, priests must keep themselves focused on their identity as men chosen and changed by God.

Cardinal Vlk had once been suspended from public ministry by the former communist government of his homeland; he took a job as a laborer and was not allowed to associate with other priests. He writes:

> Despite the awareness of being ordained for service, the priest expects himself to be a leader, and then realizes that he is not a leader if he is not listened to and followed. . . .
>
> The weakening of leadership, also on the religious and cultural level, easily calls into question the awareness of the mandate received from Jesus by means of the ordained priesthood. From this also follows an attempt to compensate by doing a volume of activities in order to feel useful; but when we realize that it takes one hundred efforts to produce only a small result, discouragement and stress arise and doubts begin: Have I been mistaken about my vocation? Is celibacy really worthwhile? Is it possible that having a family is denied to the priest . . . ?

These thoughts have passed through my mind and heart so many times, in those times when I lost all my public activities in the Church and became a layman in the eyes of many. My situation forced me to seek out my priestly identity all over again: without ministry, without visible usefulness, without being a leader. With the help of the communion of my fellow priests, after a period of painful searching, I rediscovered it. It was an immense joy to discover that Jesus arrived at the climax of his priesthood when, nailed to the cross, he could not walk, perform miracles, nor preach, but—abandoned—suffered in silence. . . . I understood and found in him my deepest priestly identity, which filled me with joy and peace. With this new priestly identity I spent ten years washing store windows on the streets of Prague.[1]

Lifted on the cross, Jesus could do nothing—nothing but abandon himself to the love and power of his Father. That's what we say we are doing (whether we are conscious of it or not) every time we kiss the altar.

A friend who is a Presbyterian minister once gave me a copy of William C. Martin's *The Art of Pastoring: Contemplative Reflections*. One chapter asks:

How would you pastor
if you could not speak?
How would you love the parish
if you were immobilized in bed?
If you can answer these questions,
you know the truth of your calling.
If you can do these things,
you will overcome all obstacles.[2]

The power of the priesthood rests in our participation in the Lord Jesus' self-emptying self-offering on the altar of the cross.

As we kiss the altar "on the outside" every day, will we also kiss it "on the inside?"

Sincerely in Christ,

+ Peter Sartain

Archbishop Peter Sartain

Notes

1. Cardinal Miloslav Vlk, "The Call of Priests to Perfection," in Congregation for the Clergy, *Priesthood: A Greater Love, International Symposium on the Thirtieth Anniversary of the Promulgation of the Conciliar Decree* Presbyterorum Ordinis (Philadelphia: Archdiocese of Philadelphia, 1997), 224–25.

2. William C. Martin, *The Art of Pastoring: Contemplative Reflections* (Pittsburgh: Vital Faith Resources, 2001), 43.

6

How a Presbyterate Prospers

Dear Brothers in the Lord,

When I joined some of my classmates for a celebration of our thirtieth anniversary of ordination, we reminisced about seminary days, caught up on what had happened through the years, and swapped funny stories. I told this one on myself:

One day shortly after I began my first assignment, we received a call that a parishioner had died, and her family requested that one of us lead the funeral rites. Having just arrived, I knew very few parishioners, but I soon learned that no one in the office knew this family. We made arrangements for the wake and funeral Mass, and I was to celebrate both.

When I arrived at the funeral home for the wake, I asked the funeral director to point out the bereaved husband. Nerves in a knot as I was about to encounter another "first," I repeatedly practiced in my head the proper words of consolation that would not only bring him peace but perhaps also bring him back to church.

Imagine my horror when, having walked across the room practicing my lines and having extended my hand in greeting, I heard myself say, "Mr. Jones, I was so happy to hear your wife died."

I learned that night that it is impossible to recover from such a blunder, no matter how hard one tries. I tripped over myself explaining that I was sad, not happy, but I had said what I had said. The grieving husband seemed to accept my clumsy apology . . . but I never saw him again.

Thinking back over the years, I can easily make a mental list of gaffes I made out of greenness, homilies that revealed my lack of life experience or lack of preparation, counseling sessions in which I was absolutely no help to those sitting before me, and funny things that happened simply because I goofed up. Many of those memories make me laugh, some embarrass me still, and all of them make me wonder at the fact that God was at work despite me.

There are some aspects of our early years of ministry which we are glad to outgrow as time goes by. Fervor, passion, and impetuosity can cause us to make fools of ourselves even when we have the best of intentions. Such was the case with a fourth-century monk by the name of Abba John.

> It is told of him that one day in his youth he said to his elder brother, "I should like to be free of all care, like the angels, who do not work, but ceaselessly offer worship to God." So he took off his cloak and went away into the desert. After a week he came back home to his brother. When he knocked on the door, he heard his brother say, before he opened it, "Who are you?" And he said, "I am John, your brother." But his brother replied, "My brother John has become like an angel, and henceforth he is no longer among men." Then John begged him to let him in, saying, "It is I." However, his brother would not let him in but left him there in distress until morning. Then, opening the door, the elder brother said to John, "You are a man and you must once again work in order to eat." Then John made a prostration before him, saying, "Forgive me."

Like all of us, Abba John had to learn that we cannot be angels when we are flesh and blood; that is not what God asks of us. But despite our youth, inexperience, sinfulness, worries, weariness, and fears, we can take God's grace seriously and allow him to do his work through us. As for Abba John, he was eventually ordained to the priesthood and became renowned for his holiness and good common sense.

The passing of years can make a great deal of difference. Observing, learning, listening, experiencing, suffering, falling down and dusting ourselves off, praying, hoping, loving: years pass, life goes on, we grow, change, and mature. Thank God! But Jesus Christ is the same yesterday, today, and forever. Thank God!

Were we called to be angels? Whatever we thought the day we entered seminary, we now know it is too late for that. We know we were called to accept as true God's baffling love for us and his wondrously wise choice of us as priests. We were called to respond by striving with every fiber of our being to immerse ourselves in Christ, to give witness to him, to gather people to him, and to feed them with the Bread of Life.

Indeed there probably are some aspects of our early years of ministry that we are glad to have outgrown—those foolish but funny things that make us smile today. However, there are probably other aspects of those early years we would do well to recover, especially that first fervor God used so powerfully to draw us close. Perhaps it was immature, unformed, and naïve, but God used it nonetheless; and it enabled us to throw ourselves trustingly into his arms.

Peter's impetuous gaffes were the flip side of his overwhelming love for the Lord—and better that he sink into the water than never follow the Lord's invitation to do the impossible. John, beloved to the Lord, ran, breathless, to see the empty tomb; his youth became the archetype of the young Church's enthusiastic, passionate love for Jesus. We would all do well to recall often the "first love"—at once fiery, inexperienced, and unsophisticated—that impelled us to say "yes" to the Lord. The rest is, literally, history. But it is the history of God at work in us.

In his later years, Abba John was to say: "A house is not built by beginning at the top and working down. You must begin with the foundations in order to reach the top." He had learned the necessity of letting God's grace transform him from within, and he knew that for grace to do its work the human heart must be humble and receptive, willing to begin again and again to ensure the foundation is strong. The years brought Abba John a simpler but more profound brand of wisdom, but he never became an angel. He learned to take God very seriously—but not himself.

In October 2008 I spent a week in Rome, not realizing until I arrived that I would be there for the thirtieth anniversary of the election of Pope John Paul II. It was a happy coincidence, because as a newly-ordained priest I had been in St. Peter's Square on the evening of October 16, 1978, and had witnessed the white smoke pouring out of the flue atop the Sistine Chapel.

I had not heard of Karol Wojtyla until that night, but many people did know him well as a man profoundly aware of his unity—his solidarity—with all of humanity by virtue of his priestly vocation.

When I arrived in Rome in October 2008, I learned by happenstance that Cardinal Stanislaw Dziwisz, Wojtyla's longtime secretary, would be celebrating an anniversary Mass in Polish at St. Peter's, and I was allowed to concelebrate. The Basilica was packed, and though I do not speak Polish I felt a special kinship with everyone there. As I processed out of the sanctuary at the end of Mass, I glanced at the vast crowd in front of me and saw a small, ordinary-looking man with a great mustache in the first pew. It was Lech Walesa.

Here was a man whose courage and concern for his brothers and sisters—his solidarity with them—had inspired him to lead their charge for freedom. Providentially, his sense of solidarity coupled with the pope's had an epoch-changing impact on the world at the end of the twentieth century. So influential was their use of the term that it became common to just about every language and eventually made its way into the Catechism.

> *Communion in charity.* In the [communion of saints], "None of us lives to himself, and none of us dies to himself" (Rom 14:7). "If one member suffers, all suffer together; if one member is honored, all rejoice together. Now you are the body of Christ and individually members of it" (1 Cor 12:26-27). "Charity does not insist on its own way" (1 Cor 13:5; cf. 10:24). In this solidarity with all men, living or dead, which is founded on the communion of saints, the least of our acts done in charity redounds to the profit of all. (953)

As members of a presbyterate, we have a distinctive reason to hold these concepts dear. Not only does our priestly vocation call us to solidarity with all people, no matter their circumstances or way of life—it also calls us to a unique and profound solidarity with one another.

Early on Jesus sent out his disciples two by two that they might give common witness to the reign of God. He had called them to leave their families, their "old" human relationships, in order to be introduced to a "new" family of his sisters and brothers. At Pentecost they were given by the Holy Spirit an even deeper communion in discipleship, a communion that was to be a mark of the Church.

We priests share the ministry of Christ, and where one of us is, there stand all of us. We do not have the same talents. We do not hold the same opinions. We do not share the same native languages or cultures. We cannot all reach all the people. But Christ comes to them through all of us, whoever and wherever one of us is. Christ is one, and through our gifts and ministry, he comes to his people and embraces them.

But Christ also comes to us priests in a unique way through the communion we have with one another. This solidarity, which is something more than fraternity, unites us spiritually and sacramentally for one another's good and growth.

As senior priests offer good example and the wisdom of the years to junior priests, so junior priests offer the inspiration of first fervor and the spontaneity of first love to senior priests. Both age and youth reveal their own kind of wisdom, and the balance is not accidental: it is the way a presbyterate prospers.

Ultimately, what matters most is not age or experience. What matters most is a common focus on Christ, fraternal charity and forgiveness, sacrificial love for our people, and our eagerness to grow in holiness as individual priests and as brothers in the Lord.

Ecce quam bonum et quam iucundum habitare fratres in unum.

> How good and how pleasant it is,
>> when brothers dwell together as one. (Ps 133:1)

Sincerely in Christ,

+ Peter Sartain

Archbishop Peter Sartain

7

In Exile

Dear Brothers in the Lord,

When Joseph was given yet another message in yet another dream—this time to flee to Egypt with his wife and newborn—I wonder what must have gone through his mind. How many more surprises, detours, and peculiarities would mark his life? Would things ever return to normal? How could he be sure he wasn't being deceived, that with good intentions he was just following the ersatz inspiration of his imagination? Joseph's share in the cross came early, anticipating the burdens his Son would bear.

The gospels don't tell us much about Joseph, but they paint the portrait of a compassionate, just, and generous man who placed his life squarely in the hands of God. None of it could have been easy, and yet we readily think of Joseph as a man at peace.

Merson's *Rest on the Flight* is one of my favorite depictions of the Holy Family's escape to Egypt. An exhausted Mary and Joseph have paused for sleep during their journey. Mary holds Jesus in her arms, and she rests on the legs of the great sphinx. Joseph, exhausted, sleeps on a mat in the sand. The somber sphinx is oblivious to the fact that it cradles the Light of the World.

Joseph was content to care for Mary and Jesus, abiding in a mystery he did not understand but accepted as God's gift and his vocation. In God's plan it was simply enough that he was there, in all his ordinariness. He was a good father and protector who had to trust that God knew

Luc-Olivier Merson, *Rest on the Flight into Egypt*, 1879. Oil on canvas, 71.8 x 128.3 cm. Museum of Fine Arts, Boston.

what he was doing through these strange events, and I think it is his peaceful acceptance that draws us to him. We have the instinctive sense that he was "in on the mystery," that is to say that he was wrapped in it and had surrendered to it. That's why he was at peace.

I'm struck by the fact that his every word to Jesus was a prayer, his every glance an act of adoration: his boy was both son and Savior.

We priests play the role of Joseph for our people, who count on us to be their fathers and protectors, similarly wrapped in the mystery. In the next few days, they will flock to church, some for their yearly visit and some perhaps for the first visit in many years. I think God is pleased they come no matter why or how long it's been, and he will use the few moments we have with them to draw them closer. Perhaps some kind of self-imposed exile has kept them away, and Joseph understands how it feels to be in confounding flight. Perhaps we don't know what words to say in order to proclaim the Christmas mystery in a way that will keep them coming back, and Joseph understands our helplessness.

Every person who will come to Mass or has been to confession in recent days is a mystery caught up in God's plan, and every priest is a Joseph, called to take up our part with devotion. We delight in the members of our family, who crowd our churches and parking lots to overflowing for a few days (and maybe test our patience!), and we recognize them as God's beloved family entrusted to us for a time to father and foster.

On the south transept of St. Raymond Nonnatus Cathedral in Joliet, an inscription above Joseph's shrine invites us to "Go to Joseph." When we go to Joseph, like Mary he points with peace to his Son—and with gentle concern for us, fathers like he, he teaches us docility to the providential plan of God.

Sincerely in Christ,

+ *Peter Sartain*

Archbishop Peter Sartain

8

Providing a Home

Dear Brothers in the Lord,

I have had the privilege of baptizing two of my great-nephews, Diego and Lucas, in my home parish, St. Paul the Apostle in Memphis. The large campus includes the "old" church (where I received my first communion and was confirmed), the "new" church (where I celebrated my first Mass, where two of my sisters were married, and where the funerals of my parents took place), the ball fields where I played as a kid, and the elementary and high schools I attended. Each time I drive onto the parish grounds, a flood of memories rushes into my head. We joined that parish when I was six years old, and it has played a pivotal role at every stage of our lives.

The baptisms were joyous occasions for my niece and her husband and the two extended families. I looked at the little ones and thought how blessed they are to be born into a family that will love them deeply and care for their every need. At this stage of their lives, Diego and Lucas are dependent on their parents absolutely—there is nothing they can do for themselves. As they grow, their parents will teach them to be less dependent for life's daily needs, and one day they will move out of their house as young men capable of caring for themselves and perhaps families of their own.

Their dependence on their parents and extended family is a lesson in itself, a hint of their absolute dependence on God. As my niece and her husband rear them to independence, a sign of their maturity will be that they realize just how dependent they are and always will be on God.

The continuity of St. Paul the Apostle Parish in the life of the Sartains has provided stability to us in good times and bad. This is a place where tears of joy and sadness were shed, where lessons were learned, where counsel was sought and given, where friendships were forged and maintained, where doubt and confusion were taken to prayer, where sins were forgiven, where spiritual battles were waged, and where vocations were inspired. It is a parish that has known its share of conflict and scandal, with parishioners who have persevered in faith and remain strong despite generational and demographic changes.

On the day of Diego's baptism, it struck me that St. Paul's is where I first learned the importance of dependence on God. It was there I learned that no matter how old I grow or how independent I regard myself, I must always be like a child in my relationship with him.

It is not easy to be childlike. Dominican Fr. Bede Jarrett (1881–1934) writes:

> Do you know he only once called them *children*? He named them apostles, he called them friends, he described one as Satan, another as a devil, he called them servants and followers: but only at the end, in John XXI, did he call them children. Through what a discipline they had passed before he gave them that name, through what failures, trials, humiliations, shocks to faith and hope, through what bleak wastes of desolation and lack of prayer, through what weariness had they to go before they became children. It's a thing one has to become . . . we pass the passion to reach childhood. It's not a condition but a goal.[1]

We pass the passion to reach childhood. Fr. Bede's insight is an important one. Spiritual childhood has to do not with naiveté but with trust, fidelity, and perseverance even in the midst of our suffering, our passion. It also evokes another passion—the passion of love. Saint Mark reports that in the agony in the Garden of Gethsemane, Jesus prayed: "Abba, Father, all things are possible to you. Take this cup away from me, but not what I will but what you will" (Mark 14:36). Although all four evangelists indicate that Jesus had often prayed to his Father ("pater" in Greek and Latin) and taught his disciples to pray likewise, it is only Mark who notes that in his passion Jesus addressed him as *Abba*, Father—the Aramaic address of a child to his dad.

We pass the passion to reach childhood. I regard the priesthood as a life of joy, and as I reflect on my experience through the years I often think of the joy our vocation has brought me. I remember the challenging times, too, and though they were certainly no fun I can see God's hand at work. He nudged me, challenged me, stretched me, awakened me— and invited me to understand better how as a priest I would always be linked to the cross of Christ. Suffering has the potential to make us bitter, cynical, and hopeless, and one might at first think that only those with adult sensibilities can navigate through it successfully. We certainly don't have to like it, much less seek it out. But when suffering enters our lives in its various forms, so do the many aspects of the passion of Jesus: trust, fidelity, perseverance, and most especially love. It was love above all that took Jesus in his passion, as a child trustingly dependent on his Father, through death to resurrection.

It is no easier for us priests than for anyone else to be childlike; perhaps in some ways it is more difficult. Still, as those joined to Jesus at the deepest level of our being, as sons of the Father and brothers to one another, our vocation calls us unremittingly in that direction: To be, with Jesus, one with the Father. To be, in Jesus, one with each other. To love, with the love of Jesus, the people we serve. To trust, with Jesus, that the Father's will is being done even if we don't understand how. To see our suffering, our passion, as joined to that of Jesus, and to know that the Father will help us through it—for our sakes and for the sakes of those to whom he sends us. To accept generously, even heroically, the crosses the Father asks us to carry as a share in his Son's passion. To be passionately childlike, fully awake to the traps and sins of this world, shrewd about the painful effects of suffering, but like children at rest in their mothers' laps. To be full of compassion, knowing through both experience and love the suffering that besets our flock.

And, yes, to be full of joy: Jesus' farewell discourse in John in the context of the Last Supper invited the disciples to enter into his mission, his suffering, and his love with trust in the Father. "I have told you this so that my joy may be in you and your joy may be complete" (cf. John 15:11; 16:24).

We pass the passion to reach childhood. It was *after* his death and resurrection that Jesus called out from the shore of the Sea of Tiberius to Peter, Thomas, Nathanael, James, John and two other disciples, "Children, have you caught anything?" We would not know Jesus if we did not know suffering. We could not be priests if we could not and did not experience suffering, for suffering joins us to his passion and the passion of the world. Ministry certainly has its discouraging, even agonizing, moments —Satan hopes we will be distracted by them thoroughly—but the things that cause us to suffer are occasions to call out uninhibitedly and without embarrassment to the one on whom we are dependent for absolutely everything: *Abba,* Father. It was thus that Jesus cried out in his hour of passion, the passion of suffering, the passion of love.

I often refer to St. Paul the Apostle in Memphis as my "home parish." It's now Diego's and Lucas's *home.* Most of us are in parish work, and it's important to keep that image in our hearts: the parishes we serve for a time are "home" to many, and the majority of them will be part of the parish much longer than we. Even if parishioners move far away, the parishes we serve always will be "home" to them. As fathers, it is our joyful privilege and vocation to provide a home in the Lord for our family, a place where his little ones, young and old, will learn to be childlike.

Sincerely in Christ,

+ *Peter Sartain*

Archbishop Peter Sartain

Note

1. Bede Bailey, Simon Tugwell, and Dom Aiden Bellenger, eds., *Letters of Bede Jarrett: letters and other papers from the English Dominican Archives* (Bath, England: Downside Abbey and Blackfriars Publications, 1989), 139–40.

9

Honoring Our Parents

Dear Brothers in the Lord,

The chalice I use most often for daily Mass was given to me many years ago by the sister of a priest-friend who died at the age of seventy-eight after a long battle with Parkinson's disease. Pat Lynch had been Director of Vocations when I entered the seminary and for the rest of his life remained a mentor and inspiration, one of three priests I consider my fathers in the priesthood. His identical twin brother, Tom, was also a priest but was killed in an automobile accident in 1961, just eleven years after their ordination. Their sister, Anita, gave me their chalices when Pat died. I gave Pat's to the Cathedral in Memphis and kept Tom's for my personal use.

Every time I use Tom's chalice I'm struck by the small diamond embedded in its base, which I believe had been part of their mother's engagement ring. The Latin inscription on the underside of the chalice reads: "Do your best all day long / Trust in God with all your heart / Take refuge in Mary with all your love / ~ Mother." I never knew their parents, but I like the fact that the fruit of their marriage—first, the friendship and guidance of Pat, and now the chalice that contains part of their rings—spills over to me even today when I celebrate Mass.

The first time I concelebrated Mass with Bishop Andrew McDonald, my predecessor in Little Rock, I noticed two wedding bands encircling the bottom of the node that connects the base to the cup of his chalice.

I also noticed that he made a point of touching the rings at the end of Mass. He explained that these were his parents' wedding bands, and the fact that they form part of his chalice is a daily reminder of their love.

When I was ordained bishop in early 2000, my mother asked what she could give me that would be significant for my ministry as bishop. I suggested a pectoral cross. When she gave me the cross, she made clear that it was a gift from both her and my father, who died in 1972. It was accompanied by her handwritten note that read, "This cross is from your dad and me. Know that whenever you wear it, we love you and are praying for you." Although I have been given several pectoral crosses, I wear that one most often. I know that my parents, now both deceased, pray for me whether I wear that cross or not, but I cherish the sense of closeness it gives me.

When I celebrate Mass in the parishes of the archdiocese, I use the chalice the parish provides, and it's obvious that often the chalice belongs to one of you, the priests who serve these parishes. It's not uncommon to see a diamond, wedding bands flattened out in the form of a cross, or an inscription honoring your parents. I always consider it a privilege to use your chalices.

Whether or not our parents' names are inscribed on our chalices or other liturgical accoutrements, and whether our parents are dead or alive, they are with us and pray for us. The sacrament of their love trained and nourished us, protected and prodded us, formed and forgave us— more often than we probably ever realized. If they are still living or lived well into their senior years, we might find ourselves in a position similar to that of many of our parishioners—being caregiver and guide to the ones who gave us life. In my mother's later years, my sisters liked to remind me that she looked to me for the final word, though I was the youngest. "You know, of course, that it's not okay with mom until *you* say it's okay," one of them once told me, with a hint of sarcasm.

We priests come from a variety of families. Some of us were born into large families, others into small. Some of us grew up in happy families, others in pained and suffering families. Some of our families did not have to be concerned about money; others pinched every penny and struggled endlessly, even unsuccessfully, to make ends meet. Some of us had our parents well into old age, others for only a few years, and some of us never knew the parents of our birth.

Just like us, our parents had feet of clay, and at some point in our lives we had to come to terms with their faults and shortcomings, just as they had to come to terms with ours. Most likely, our personal genealogies read like that of Jesus at the beginning of Matthew, with ups, downs, heroes, crooks, champions, and cheats. When I became chaplain of a village for seniors in the 1980s, one of the residents came to the sacristy immediately after the first Mass I offered there. She was excited to announce that she had known my father's brother many years earlier. "He ran off with my niece," she said with a smile. He was married at the time, and neither the marriage nor the dishonest romance lasted. (But in an act of reconciliation and fidelity that my mother later reported to us with great admiration, the wife my uncle had betrayed many years earlier took care of him when he was dying of cancer.)

I write these simple words to honor our parents and those others whom God sent into our lives to father and mother us. Alive or dead, they love us and pray for us, and I consider them an important part of our presbyteral family. They gave us life in more ways than we can count, and our love for them gives us strength. May God bless them, console them, heal them, and give them eternal rest.

> Listen to your father who begot you,
>   and despise not your mother when she is old.
> Buy truth and do not sell:–
>   wisdom, instruction, understanding!
> The father of a just person will exult greatly;
>   whoever begets a wise son will rejoice in him.
> Let your father and mother rejoice;
>   let her who bore you exult. (Prov 23:22-26)

> Receive, O Lord, the sacrifice we offer you
> for my father and mother (our parents);
> grant them everlasting joy in the land of the living
> and unite me (us) with them
> in the happiness of the Saints.
> Through Christ our Lord. (Prayer over the Offerings during a Mass
>   "For the Priest's Parents" in the Roman Missal)

Sincerely in Christ,

+ Peter Sartain

Archbishop Peter Sartain

10

In Love with God

Dear Brothers in the Lord,

While home in Tennessee on vacation, I learned that a good friend and seminary classmate, Joe Tagg, had died in his sleep of an apparent heart attack. Joe did a great deal of good as a priest, and the cathedral was packed to overflowing with those who had personally experienced his impact. His journey to the priesthood had been, to say the least, an adventure.

Reared in an upper-class Memphis society family with deep roots in the Church, Joe was a colorful character who loved sports, people, and fun. At the University of Tennessee during the 1960s he served as vice president of the student body and president of his fraternity. He hosted a sports show on a Knoxville radio station, *The Jumpin' Joe Tagg Show*. After graduation he took a job at a bank, attended law school at night, and in a few years began a lucrative law practice. He liked to say, "I'm just a west Tennessee do-right who occasionally does wrong." Once he appeared on the old TV show *What's My Line*—his line being that he was an attorney who owned a pickle factory—but that's another story. In fact, with Joe there was always "another story," the latest invariably more fascinating than the last—and all of them true.

Since childhood Joe had entertained thoughts of the priesthood, and in 1974 he took the leap and entered first theology with me. His wit and charm, his larger-than-life persona, his down-home southern way of dispensing pearls of wisdom, and his genuine piety won the hearts of many—including that of a young woman from Memphis who came to visit Rome with her family during our fourth year.

We had been ordained deacons with our class in April 1977 and were slated to be ordained priests in Memphis in July 1978. On the Tuesday before our ordination, Joe asked to see me. We stepped into a conference room at the chancery and he said, "Peter, I've decided not to be ordained. I've met a girl and want to pursue the relationship."

You can imagine the courage it took for him to make this admission so close to ordination as well as the apprehension it caused in my final days of preparation. Last-minute changes had to be made in the liturgy and a myriad of other plans, but the ordination went off without a glitch. Joe was present, class act that he was.

Thus I began my life as a priest, and he returned to the practice of law. Within a few years, his relationship with the young woman had run its course, and he went about his work, faithful to daily Mass and prayer. We kept in close touch all the while. Joe had always nurtured a devotion to the Sacred Heart of Jesus and the Immaculate Heart of Mary, and while in New Orleans for the 1987 Sugar Bowl, he prayed for direction before a favorite statue of the Sacred Heart. Not long after returning home, he was asked to assist the family of a priest who had died of a heart attack while visiting Memphis. Collecting the priest's belongings, he watched a Sacred Heart badge fall to the floor at his feet and saw it as another nudge from the Lord. Soon thereafter he confessed to me that he was thinking of asking to be ordained a priest after all. We had many conversations about what had changed and why he now felt ready, and it became clear that what he was feeling was authentic discernment, the work of the Holy Spirit.

Together we went to see the bishop, and I'll never forget our simple conversation walking up the steps to the bishop's home. He said, "Peter, I don't know how else to describe what's happened in my relationship with God. All I can say is, it's like falling in love."

Ten and one-half years after he had decided to withdraw from ordination, Joe was ordained a priest. He asked me to preach his first Mass, a privilege I eagerly accepted. I spoke about falling in love with God. In his twenty-two years as a priest, Joe served as parochial vicar, pastor of two parishes, and, after completing his JCL, Judicial Vicar. He was a popular retreat director, confessor, and all-around good guy who could be counted on for a colorful, pithy phrase that said what needed to be said.

Like all of us, Joe was not without his quirks, some of them endearing (he had a fondness for expensive Gucci shoes but rarely wore socks) and others surprising (he was as picky as any child about his food), but he loved the Lord deeply. As both lawyer and priest he always had extra time for the poor and downtrodden, and he taught the rich to love the poor. He kept his countless deeds of mercy secret unless he needed the help of people of means. Once, after spotting a poor man with one leg on the street—a complete stranger—he introduced himself and asked the man if he would like to have a new leg. He then collected money from friends to have the man fitted with a costly prosthesis. Joe ministered with extraordinary generosity until his unexpected death on March 19, 2011, his patronal feast.

March 19 was also a pivotal day in the life of Thomas Merton. On that day in 1958, Merton had an epiphany that he described in a journal and later in *Conjectures of a Guilty Bystander*. He wrote:

> In Louisville, at the corner of Fourth and Walnut, in the center of the shopping district, I was suddenly overwhelmed with the realization that I loved all those people, that they were mine and I theirs, that we could not be alien to one another even though we were total strangers. . . .
>
> I have the immense joy of being man, a member of a race in which God Himself became incarnate. As if the sorrows and stupidities of the human condition could overwhelm me, now that I realize what we all are. And if only everybody could realize this! But it cannot be explained. There is no way of telling people that they are all walking around shining like the sun. This changes nothing in the sense and value of my solitude, for it is in fact the function of solitude to make one realize such things with a clarity that would be impossible to anyone completely immersed in the other cares, the other illusions, and all the automatisms of a tightly collective existence. My solitude, however, is not my own, for I see now how much it belongs to them—and that I have a responsibility for it in their regard, not just in my own. It is because I am one with them that I owe it to them to be alone, and when I am alone, they are not "they" but my own self. There are no strangers![1]

Joe's experience helped me understand that if I do not allow myself to be naked and vulnerable before God, I will not fall in love with God. If I am not in love with God, I will not hear his call or persevere in answering that call. If I am not in love with God, I will not live my life such that I seek to please him in all things. If I am not in love with God, I will not pray from the depths of my heart. If I am not in love with God, my fear will get the best of me when times get tough—and times will get tough. If I am not in love with God, I will never be filled with wonder and awe that he has called me, and I will not be humble enough to trust him completely come what may.

Similarly, Thomas Merton's experience helped him to understand that if he never grasped that these people—all people—belong to God and are loved by God, he would never truly love them. He might serve them well, with dedication and long hours of expert ministry. He might be filled with genuine altruism and affection for them, with concern for their human rights and well-being. But he might not love them as God loves them, with God's love, because God loves them, and because God had sent him to love them. If he did not love them as God loves them, he would never understand that everything about his vocation was *for them* and would never learn to give himself as a sacrifice with Jesus *for them.*

I was blessed with parents and priestly models who by example awakened in me a love for God that gradually, by God's grace, developed into falling in love with God. Nonetheless I had the disappointing suspicion throughout seminary that I did not love others as I should if I wanted to be a good priest. I prayed that I would, that God would plant such love in my heart, and after ordination I went about priestly tasks as lovingly as I could. Through the joys and struggles—particularly of those early years—God answered my prayers without my knowing it.

Eventually I also had a "Fourth and Walnut" epiphany. Mine was at a dinner celebrating the induction of new members of a Hall of Fame for the local Catholic boys' high school. I was seated at the head table before several hundred people, many of whom I knew from the parish. In the flash of an instant it occurred to me: I *love* these people. I did not know them all, but I loved them all. I recognized that God had answered my prayers, and from that moment God enabled me to embrace his people in a new way because he showed me that it was with His love that I was to love them.

The witness to *communio* given by mature priests is a critical, much-needed witness in the modern world. Given the challenges faced by disintegrating families, the isolation experienced by many for a variety of reasons, and the narcissistic nature of many lifestyles, the community life created by a priest offers a countercultural and uniquely compelling response to the questions of many people. A mature priest creates and nurtures a profound experience of communion and reconciliation, stability and fidelity, and the expression of the deepest human vocation—to love. That vocation, as all vocations, comes from the heart of God.

Pope John Paul II wrote in *Pastores Dabo Vobis:*

> People need to come out of their anonymity and fear. They need to be known and called by name, to walk in safety along the paths of life, to be found again if they have become lost, to be loved, to receive salvation as the supreme gift of God's love. All this is done by Jesus, the Good Shepherd—by himself and by his priests with him. (82)

Seminarians need to learn to be fathers who fall in love with God and love those God loves, who learn to sacrifice themselves with and through Jesus for the evangelization of the world. They must be helped to see that in our struggles God is teaching us to love, that he is drawing out of our depths the resources he himself has given us, so that we will love him and his people *from there.*

In separate addresses to seminarians, Pope Benedict XVI said:

> The seminarian experiences the beauty of that call in a moment of grace which could be defined as "falling in love." His soul is filled with amazement, which makes him ask in prayer: "Lord, why me?" But love knows no "why"; it is a free gift to which one responds with the gift of self. (World Youth Day 2005)

> I urge you [seminarians] to deepen your friendship with Jesus, the Good Shepherd. Talk heart to heart with him. Reject any temptation to ostentation, careerism, or conceit. Strive for a pattern of life truly marked by charity, chastity and humility, in imitation of Christ, the Eternal High Priest, of whom you are to become living icons. Dear seminarians, I pray for you daily. Remember that what counts before the Lord is to dwell in his love and to make his love shine forth for others. (New York, 2008)

Joseph Laughlin Tagg III sought to be formed by the Hearts of Jesus and Mary, to learn the lessons God desired to teach him, and to share those lessons with those God sent him to love. His road to the priesthood was uniquely his, and he walked it courageously and boldly, if a bit hesitantly at first. When he surrendered to God who loves him, he became fully himself. Along the way, he manifested God's love to the poor and brought countless souls to Christ. I was blessed to be his friend.

If, then, I am no longer
seen or found on the common,
you will say that I am lost;
that, stricken by love,
I lost myself and was found.[2]

Sincerely in Christ,

+ Peter Sartain

Archbishop Peter Sartain

Note

1. Thomas Merton, *Conjectures of a Guilty Bystander* (Garden City, NY: Image Books, 1968), 153–55.

2. John of the Cross, *Spiritual Canticle*, in *The Collected Works of St. John of the Cross*, rev. ed., trans. Kieran Kavanaugh and Otilio Rodriguez (Washington, DC: ICS Publications, 1991), stanza 29.

PRIESTLY PRACTICALITIES

11

It's Not about Me

Dear Brothers in the Lord,

The last time I wore a tuxedo was March 3, 1973, when I walked my sister, Sally, down the long aisle of St. Paul the Apostle Church in Memphis for her marriage to Art. Having raised four children, she and Art are now enjoying three grandchildren. Art is a retired pharmacist and parish volunteer, and Sally is hard at work as principal of a Catholic high school for girls. I have had the privilege of baptizing two of their grandsons in the very church in which they were married.

I have learned a great deal about love, commitment, and sacrifice from my family, and the lessons continue. Recently all of us discussed the possibility of traveling to Rome for the liturgy during which I would receive the pallium from Pope Benedict XVI. After a phone conversation about the trip, Sally wrote a follow-up e-mail, in which she explained that she couldn't sacrifice the time away from her husband:

> There are many things at play in this decision, which I made on my own. For a lot of reasons, it just doesn't feel right for me right now. I get 4 weeks vacation a year, which sounds like a lot, until you consider that administrators take vacation at Christmas or spring break. Vacation time that I use for just me, out of town, is vacation time I don't get to spend with Art and that I won't get to make up to him. He didn't say "no" and would never say that. But he was

> relieved tonight when I told him I'd decided not to do it, and that
> told me what I needed to know from him.
>
> I know it will be a wonderful experience and know that I will feel a
> little twinge of regret when June rolls around and I'm not there. I
> would love to go, really, if it was just me. But I'm not "just me" and
> haven't been for 38 years (can you believe that? 38 years?). So I made
> this decision for the "we" and not for the "me."

Our parents had a strong, faith-filled, faithful love for one another and for us—a faith that placed them daily in the position of making decisions for the "we" and not for the "me," a faith that arose from their commitment to one another but had its origin in God's faithfulness. Isn't it that way with every vocation? Once accepted, a vocation impels us to live for the sake of—and in communion with—others, for the glory of God. It is no longer about "me" but "we"—or better, "You."

Those who wittingly or unwittingly make themselves the center of the universe are not happy, and everyone in their vicinity feels the unpleasant tug of their gravity. The one who talks incessantly about his or her accomplishments or woes quickly becomes a bore and misses the opportunity for authentic relationships. Life is not all about "me." Marriage, if it is a merger of egos—a merger of "me's"—will fail. Ministry, if it is about "me," is no longer ministry. The Lord's way draws us out of ourselves and teaches us the way of surrender to the other.

Hebrews 11 extols the faithful love of a band of Old Testament heroes and heroines who accepted their vocation, took God at his word, and kept *their* word, especially when times were tough and the future seemed foggy. Like Abraham, they "went forth" based on a promise of faithfulness, and their own response of faithfulness enabled them to see and do things otherwise unimaginable. In each instance Hebrews presents for our reflection, there is a "we" aspect of God's call and the person's response. Each was called to let go of "me" and surrender to God for the sake of the people God loved.

Through baptism a definitive change happened within us by participation in the death and resurrection of Jesus. "I have been crucified with Christ; yet I live, no longer I, but Christ lives in me" (Gal 2:19-20). Our "I" has been joined to and overtaken by Christ—not first because *we* chose to give ourselves to him but because *he* gave himself for us. In effect, at baptism we entered into a new way of living marked not by self-seeking or self-proving, not by shame or knee-jerk defenses for our misdeeds, but by receiving ourselves back—justified and forgiven—from

Christ. For every Christian, the old "I" of self-*seeking* is conquered by the self-*giving* of Jesus.

We priests are called not only to free ourselves of self-absorption in a psychological sense but even to surrender our "I" to God to be used completely and irrevocably by his Son. Still, in our priestly ministry we often say "I," "my," and "me."

"*I* baptize you," "*I* absolve you from your sins." "For this is *my* body, which will be given up for you. This is the cup of *my* blood, the blood of the new and eternal covenant. . . . Do this in memory of *me*." Even when the word is not there explicitly, it is there implicitly. The "I" of the priest is at work in every sacrament, in preaching the Word, in the ministry of charity and in every priestly act; but the "I" of the priest is not his personally. It is the "I" of Christ, for it is he who is at work in us, he who loves his people through us, he who shepherds the flock for whom he gave his life. When we say "I" in ministry, Christ is the "I" who is speaking.

In his Chrism Mass homily in 2006, Pope Benedict said that the priesthood of the Old Covenant became something entirely new in Christ:

> He alone can say: "This is my Body . . . this is my Blood." The mystery of the priesthood of the Church lies in the fact that we, miserable human beings . . . can speak with his "I": in persona Christi. He wishes to exercise his priesthood through us.

John reports that during the Feast of Tabernacles Jesus went to the temple and began to preach to people who were amazed that he taught the Scriptures like a rabbi without having studied under a rabbi. He answered, "My teaching is not my own but is from the one who sent me" (John 7:16). In a 1990 *Communio* article ("Concerning the Notion of Person in Theology"), then-Cardinal Ratzinger explained that in the ancient Jewish mindset, an emissary is not important in himself but stands with the sender and is one with the sender. "John extends this Jewish idea of mission . . . by depicting Christ as *the* emissary who is in his entire nature 'the one sent.'" He mentions Augustine's commentary on Christ's ambiguous statement, "*My* teaching is *not* my teaching."

> Augustine offers a marvelous commentary on this text by asking: Is this not a contradiction? It is either my teaching or not. He finds an answer in the statement, Christ's doctrine is he himself, and he himself is not his own, because his "I" exists entirely from the "you."

> He goes on to say . . . "what belongs to you as much as your 'I,' and what belongs to you as little as your 'I?'" Your "I" is on the one hand what is most your own and at the same time what you have least of yourself; it is most of all not your own, because it is only from the "you" that it can exist as an "I" in the first place.[1]

In baptism we received ourselves back from Christ no longer enslaved to endless, futile, bungled attempts at self-justification. In holy orders, we were overtaken by Christ in an additional way, ourselves now being sent by the One Who Was Sent. "As the Father has sent me, so I send you" (John 20:21).

A priest pronounces the words of Jesus, not as one who merely quotes a famous person (the folks at the Feast of Tabernacles were accustomed to rabbis quoting other rabbis), but as his very breath and voice, his instrument, through whom he addresses his people. Our "I" is his "I." Because of ordination, the "I" of the Lord Jesus is always at work in us, even when we are not directly engaged in priestly duties. And because with Jesus everything is directed toward the glory of his Father, his "I" is at the same time always "You." So it is with us.

Hundreds of thousands of people have sought us out for sacraments, blessings, counsel, support, encouragement, and all manner of spiritual care. Each time they have encountered Christ himself. It is an interesting but telling fact that when an ordained minister gives a blessing, he does not say, "May Almighty God bless us." Rather, he says, "May Almighty God bless you." The reason is that the "I" who is God is blessing the "you" who are his people.

In recent years I have tried to be more attentive and intentional than I was in the past when offering blessings to those who ask for them. I give many blessings, and given the setting in which they usually take place (receptions, noisy rooms, parking lots) it is not always easy to concentrate. I have realized, however, that there is great power (the power of the cross and resurrection) and infinite love (the love of God poured out in Jesus) in a priestly blessing. I try to be actively and personally present to those who ask for the blessing. I try to recall that I am praising (blessing) God for his favor, begging him to shed that favor on those before me, and asking him to dispose them to receive his favor—and all of this with the "I" who is Christ offering everything to the "You" who is his Father. Many people are not bashful about asking for a blessing, but others are, and I try to be discerning of those who hope to receive one but remain silent: "May I give you a blessing?"

The witnesses extolled by Hebrews still speak to us by their ageless testimony. They were like you and me, like our parents—ordinary folks gifted with faith in the eternal God. It was their faith—or, rather, it was the God who gave them faith—that enabled them to persevere, because in some way they "saw" what they hoped for. It was faith that perked their ears to hear things heard only by those who revere God, faith that caused them to do things that made some shake their heads in disbelief (think of Noah, who at God's command built an ark to save his people). It was faith that helped them go forth, and keep going forth, on the basis of God's imprecise promise. It was faith that sharpened their vision to see beyond the struggles of the day all the way to the land of promise. It was faith that emboldened then to believe that the impossible is possible with God.

Those who trust in God's fidelity and have become faithful in return persevere in hardship, jump back on their feet when they have stumbled, and (most important of all) never go back on a promise. When they make a decision, it is no longer about "me" but "we" and "You." This is a beautiful, mysterious, and curiously, even baffling aspect of fidelity. Making decisions based on "we" impels us to do what might seem illogical, inconvenient, inefficient, and counterintuitive to others. I remember well as a kid watching my parents make such decisions, and, though I shook my head then, I thank God now. It was not so in every family in our neighborhood.

God does not maneuver, posture, or back away from his promises. His love is so faithful that it endures to the end, even to the end that was the seeming absurdity of the cross. There were those like Peter who disagreed with Jesus about the need for him to suffer. Oddly and ironically, when Peter said to Jesus, "God forbid, Lord! No such thing shall ever happen to you," he was trying to convince him not to be *that* faithful or *that* generous. There must be an easier way, a more benign means of fulfilling the promise; perhaps a way of fulfilling my hope that would be a little less demanding . . . of *me*.

Pope Benedict's 2006 homily for the ordination of priests has always touched me, ever since a brief quotation from it was included in a homemade Easter card I once received from friends. I close this letter with some excerpts from that homily and a little prayer of my own.

> Day after day it is necessary to learn that I do not possess my life for myself. Day by day I must learn to abandon myself; to keep myself available for whatever he, the Lord, needs of me at a given

moment, even if other things seem more appealing and more important to me: it means giving life, not taking it. It is in this very way that we experience freedom: freedom from ourselves, the vastness of being. . . .

When [those entrusted to our care] realize that someone is speaking only in his own name and drawing from himself alone, they guess that he is too small and cannot be what they are seeking; but wherever another's voice re-echoes in a person, the voice of the Creator, of the Father, the door opens to the relationship for which the person is longing. . . .

However, it is only possible [to "know" our people] properly if the Lord has opened our hearts, if our knowing does not bind people to our own small, private self, to our own small heart, but rather makes them aware of the Heart of Jesus, the Heart of the Lord. It must be knowing with the Heart of Jesus, oriented to him, a way of knowing that does not bind the person to me but guides him or her to Jesus, thereby making one free and open.[2]

† † †

Lord Jesus,

I am often in your way,

and for that I bow my head

and seek your gentle mercy.

Free me from self-seeking and anxiety about myself.

Free me of vain concerns that divert my attention

when I should be focused on You and the one before me.

When the homily is about to begin and after it has ended,

may my only desire be to proclaim You.

When faced with worrisome challenges,

may my only concern be that with You I do the Father's will.

When troubled by a thousand distractions

may I remember that they were all resolved on your Cross.

When burdened by responsibility,

may I trust in You at work in me.

When tempted by conceit or deceit,

may I be humble, giving your Father the praise.

When dulled by weariness or sluggishness

may I be swift to respond to the cries of your people.

Help me to get out of the way, Lord Jesus,

and disappear into You,

that You alone will be revealed.

Though there is nothing that belongs more to me than my "I,"

there is nothing that belongs as little to me as my "I."

It is Yours, Lord Jesus—

I am Yours, Lord Jesus—

to do with as You will for the blessing of Your Father

and the loving of those You love.

Amen.

Sincerely in Christ,

+ Peter Sartain

Archbishop Peter Sartain

Notes

1. Joseph Cardinal Ratzinger, "Retrieving the Tradition: Concerning the notion of person in theology," *Communio* 17 (1990): 446–47.

2. Pope Benedict XVI, Homily for the Holy Mass for the Ordination to the Priesthood of 15 Deacons of the Diocese of Rome, Vatican Basilica, May 7, 2006.

12

In Our Labor, Rest Most Sweet

The meaning of the Sabbath is to celebrate time rather than space. Six days a week we live under the tyranny of things of space; on the Sabbath we try to become attuned to holiness in time. It is a day on which we are called upon to share in what is eternal in time, to turn from the results of creation to the mystery of creation; from the world of creation to the creation of the world.

—Abraham Joshua Heschel[1]

Dear Brothers in the Lord,

A priest friend once told me that a pastor in his diocese complained that his new parochial vicar had arrived "without batteries." In seminary he been taught to take care of himself, but he had taken the lesson to the extreme: that's all he did.

These days, we are acutely aware of the tightness of our priest personnel situation and the growing populations of our dioceses with their accompanying pastoral needs. The temptation is to assume that the solution is to work more hours, but in the process we neglect the Lord—and ourselves.

I hesitate to write about "taking care of ourselves," because the phrase is often overused. We know it is important to make time for retreat and vacation, but we have all worried about the stack of mail and messages that will greet us upon our return; we have wondered if it will be possible to arrange coverage for the parish in our absence; we have failed to plan our schedules far enough in advance; we feel a compulsive need to stay in touch while away in case of emergency. Even with such concerns (which are often, quite frankly, excuses in disguise), it is important to take care of ourselves, lest we lose ourselves—and not in the sense that the Lord taught.

This was a lesson the desert fathers understood well. In their case, there was a keen awareness that the point of their way of life was not asceticism for the sake of asceticism. If asceticism became the goal, then God was no longer the goal, and the ascetic life was misdirected. Theirs was a life of "striving," but not to the point of keeping an unhealthy tension, like a continuously taut rope.

> It was said of Anthony that one day he was relaxing with the brothers outside the cell when a hunter came by and rebuked him. Anthony said, "Bend your bow and shoot an arrow," and he did so. "Bend it again and shoot another," and he did—and again and again. The hunter said, "Father, if I keep my bow always stretched it will break." "So it is with the monk," replied Anthony; "if we push ourselves beyond measure we will break; it is right for us from time to time to relax our efforts."[2]

We want to be healthy in body, mind, and soul, and there are many reasons and many means to take care of ourselves. At a bare minimum, we should take a day off each week, a good vacation each year, an annual retreat, and undergo an annual physical examination. We need to be away from our assignments to clear out the cobwebs and bask in the Lord's goodness. Most of us could say there is never an end to the work on our dockets, but we must be careful not to succumb to the illusion that we can get everything done. We must step off the treadmill regularly, deliberately, and without guilt. It is crucial that we take time for prayer, for rest, for activities that relax and refresh, and for extended time with family and friends. We must let God fill us so we will have something to give to others and to ourselves. If we never get off the treadmill, the world will pass us by—though we were thinking all along that we were the only ones moving.

Among its many layers of meaning, the Sabbath was a celebration of God's covenant with Israel and his never-failing care. Since abstention from work was fundamental to Sabbath observance, during the Israelites' sojourn in the wilderness God miraculously provided a double portion of manna on Friday so that they would not be forced to gather food on the Sabbath. On their day of holiness and rest, God still supplied their needs.

Early Christian writers adopted pre-Christian terms relating to "rest"—such as the Greek *hesychia* (stillness, rest) and its Latin equivalent, *quies*, as well as *otium* (leisure, with its good and bad aspects) and *vacare* (to be free from occupation), and deepened their meaning. To their spiritual vocabulary they added *Sabbath* and *requies*. *Requies* is a particularly interesting term meaning "rest" or "repose from labor, suffering, and care"; and in biblical thought, *requies* is even seen as a goal. God rested after creation (Gen 2:2), and Israel participated in this rest through the Sabbath. God promised rest to his people (Exod 30:14). Jesus promised rest to those who come to him (Matt 11:29), and ultimately those who die in the Lord will find rest from their labors (Rev 14:13).[3] Augustine announces a major theme of his *Confessions* (that the human vocation can be summed up in terms of *requies*) with these famous words: "You stir man to take pleasure in praising you, because you have made us for yourself, and our heart is restless until it rests in you."[4] The Sequence of Pentecost uses *requies* to describe the Holy Spirit: *In labore requies* is poetically rendered as "In our labor, rest most sweet."

Toward the end of his life, St. Bernard of Clairvaux witnessed the coronation of one of his own monks, Bernardo Pignatelli, as Pope Eugene III. As a means of offering support and advice to his former student, Bernard wrote *Five Books On Consideration*, which offered practical counsel on matters pertaining to the pope's life and ministry—everything from recognizing the importance of prayer to dealing with the people of Rome, balancing a hectic schedule, and relating to passive-aggressive coworkers.[5]

Bernard warns Eugene not to succumb to relentless busyness to the neglect of prayer and leisure. Of particular concern to Bernard is that Eugene will become so accustomed to a hectic schedule that he will become calloused and unreflective. This way of life, Bernard suggests, leads not to inner peace but to hardness of heart. It is worth quoting him at length:

> I am afraid that you will despair of an end to the many demands that are made upon you and become calloused and gradually suppress your sense of just and useful pain. It would be much wiser to remove yourself from these demands even for a while, than to allow yourself to be distracted by them and led, little by little, where you certainly do not want to go. Where? To a hard heart. Do not go on to ask what that is; if you have not been terrified by it, it is yours already. A hard heart is precisely one which does not shudder at itself because it is insensitive. . . .

It is not the virtue of patience to permit yourself to be enslaved when you can be free. Do not fool yourself: this is servitude to which you are surely being brought as the days go by. It is the sign of a dull heart not to sense your own continual affliction. . . .

Are you less a slave because you serve not one but all?

If you want to belong totally to all men in the likeness of him who was made all things to all men [1 Cor 9:22], I praise your devotion to humanity, but only if it be complete. Now, how can it be complete when you have excluded yourself? You too are a man. For your devotion to be whole and complete, let yourself be gathered into that bosom which receives everyone. Otherwise, as the Lord says, "What does it profit you to gain the whole world, but lose yourself alone?" Now, since everyone possesses you, make sure that you too are among the possessors. Why should you be cheated of your service? How long will you be like the wind which passes by but never returns [Psalm 77:39]? How long will you refuse to receive yourself with the others even when it is your turn? . . . The fool and the wise man, the slave and the free man, the rich and the poor man, man and woman, the old and the young, cleric and layman, the just and the impious, all equally share you; they all drink from the public fountain of your breast, and will you stand aside thirsting?

Let your waters be dispersed in the street. . . . But you also drink with the others from the waters of your own well. . . . If you are a stranger to yourself, to whom are you not? If a man is no use to himself, to whom is he useful?[6]

Bernard recognized these dangers in his own life and that of the pope, but his caveat applies to every person in every occupation. It is ironic that the very work we undertake for the good of others can—if we are not careful—be the cause of our neglecting them. Thus there is another reason for priests to take care of ourselves, perhaps the most important reason of all: *our poverty.*

Being a priest is not first and foremost about having a well-honed skill, a brain full of book learning, or the wisdom of experience. It is first and foremost about Christ working within and through us. It is about Christ overtaking us. It is about our personal conversion. Thus we must first admit our absolute poverty and offer ourselves to him as empty and open vessels.

Paradoxically, asking priests to take care of ourselves is another way of inviting us to be detached from ourselves. When we become too fatigued and anxious about the unmet needs of ministry, we become narcissistic without realizing it. Moreover, fatigue can cause resentment and bitterness, and like Martha we begin to think that we are the only ones working while everyone else is relaxing. Taking care of ourselves keeps us both other-centered and God-centered.

Saint Bernard adds an interesting twist to the story of Martha and Mary in his second Sermon for the Assumption. He comments on Matthew 12:43-45, when Jesus says:

> When an unclean spirit goes out of a person it roams through arid regions searching for rest [Vulgate: *quaerens requiem*] but finds none. Then it says, "I will return to my home from which I came." But upon returning, it finds it empty, swept clean, and put in order. Then it goes and brings back with itself seven other spirits more evil than itself, and they move in and dwell there; and the last condition of that person is worse than the first. Thus it will be with this evil generation.

Jesus' comment that the person cleansed from the evil spirit is a home "empty, swept clean and put in order" reminds Bernard of the story of Martha and Mary. He sees the regular observance of monastic life as Martha's role of "sweeping" the house and, playing on the meaning of "vacare," he sees Mary's role as that of "filling" the house: "Her time is left vacant to attend to the Lord so that the house itself may not be left vacant by him."[7] Here it is also interesting to note that Jesus makes it clear that the unclean spirit looks for *requiem* but cannot find it: evil cannot find rest because it will not rest in God.

Admitting our poverty, standing consciously empty before God, and learning to be detached from ourselves is the best way to find peace and serenity in the midst of ministry's demands and in any storm. It is also the best way to guard against narcissism, resentment, bitterness, and surrender to evil. It is a way of allowing our house to be filled and thus, at the deepest of levels, it is the best way to rest: *in the Lord*.

Building on insights from ancient spiritual writers and others such as John of the Cross, Blessed Elizabeth of the Trinity (1880–1906) offers a unique and helpful image. In a poem about the Incarnation, she writes:

> There is One who knows all mysteries
> And who embraced them from Eternity:
> And this same One . . . the Father's Word he is . . .
> See that One come, with Love's excess . . .
>
> His sanctuary, I! He rests in me—
> There is the peace one looks for and attains . . .

When I first read Blessed Elizabeth's poem, I thought of the account of Jesus sleeping in a boat as he and his disciples crossed the Sea of Galilee in a violent storm. It occurred to me that Jesus, who rests in his Father, rests in me as well. The boat in which he sleeps is the one that sailed the Sea of Galilee, but it is also the boat that is my soul, my life. Saint Paul (whom she called the father of her soul) had taught Blessed Elizabeth that we are God's temple ("His sanctuary, I!"). If God has chosen to make his home in us, to rest in us, there is no reason to fear, though the wind should blow and the waves crash about. Jesus, with total confidence in the Father, rests in me, so that I may be at peace in him. "There is the peace one looks for and attains . . ."

Brothers in the Lord, if you feel the wind and waves but not the peace of Jesus at rest, remember that you, too, are his chosen sanctuary. Jesus, who rests in the Father—*because he rests in the Father*—rests in you.

Ministry is participation in Christ's work of re-creation, and here is where we must remind ourselves that he is in charge, and we are not. We cannot do or finish everything, but he can and will, in his good time, in his wise way. If we neglect him, our loved ones, and ourselves, we will sadly discover that we have logged many miles on the treadmill but gone nowhere, clocked many hours on the job but accomplished little. Just as our ministry is a participation in God's work, so is our rest a participation in God's rest. Ultimately, then, ministry is not about my *effort* but my *rest* in God, who is always both at work and at rest in me.

Saint Bernard writes to Pope Eugene:

> Do you think you can find work to be done in the field of your Lord? Much indeed. Certainly the Prophets could not correct everything. They left something for their sons, the Apostles, to do; and they, your parents, have left something for you. But you cannot do everything. For you will leave something to your successor, and he to others, and they to others until the end of time."[8]

. . .

> And so, I say, you do your part and God will take care of his satisfactorily without your worry and anxiety. Plant, water, be concerned, and you have done your part. To be sure, God, not you, will give the growth when he wishes.[9]

You might need rest after reading this long letter! These many words are meant as a way of saying that I hope your ministry has ample room for prayer and rest. May God recharge your batteries, rekindle your enthusiasm in ministry, refill your houses swept clean by grace, re-enliven your appreciation of the mystery of creation, and renew you for his work of re-creation in Christ Jesus.

"See that One come, with Love's excess!" *Requiescamus in eo.*

Sincerely in Christ,

+ *Peter Sartain*

Archbishop Peter Sartain

Notes

1. Abraham Joshua Heschel, *The Sabbath* (New York: Farrar, Straus and Giroux, 1951), 10.

2. Benedicta Ward, SLG, *The Sayings of the Desert Fathers: The Alphabetical Collection* (Kalamazoo: Cistercian Publications, 1984), xxiii.

3. See Edith Scholl, OCSO, *Words for the Journey: A Monastic Vocabulary* (Collegeville, MN: Cistercian Publications, 2009), 42–55.

4. Augustine, *The Confessions,* trans. Henry Chadwick, Oxford World's Classics (Oxford: Oxford University Press, 1992), 3.

5. Bernard of Clairvaux, *Five Books on Consideration: Advice to a Pope,* trans. John D. Anderson and Elizabeth T. Kennan, The Works of Bernard of Clairvaux, vol. 13, Cistercian Fathers 37 (Kalamazoo, MI: Cistercian Publications, 1976).

6. Ibid., 27–34

7. Bernard of Clairvaux, qtd. in Scholl, *Words for the Journey,* 54.

8. Bernard of Clairvaux, *Five Books on Consideration,* 57.

9. Ibid., 112.

13

Gracefully Dealing with Alexander the Coppersmith

Dear Brothers in the Lord,

I have always been intrigued by Paul's comment toward the end of his second letter to Timothy: "Alexander the coppersmith did me a great deal of harm; the Lord will repay him according to his deeds" (2 Tim 4:14).

What intrigues me is that Paul inserts this very personal statement in the middle of final admonitions about perseverance in preaching "whether it is convenient or inconvenient," when people are lured away and "diverted to myths," and when there is hardship (2 Tim 4:2-4). It was always a tragedy when people like Alexander rejected the Gospel; however, here there is a hint that it was not only the Gospel that was being rejected but also Paul himself. Whatever the harm done by Alexander, it stung in a personal way.

Our experience is not that different from Paul's. With sadness we hear of parishioners who have left the church repulsed by scandal, lured away by a gospel of prosperity, seduced by evil, or motivated by some unspoken cause. We hear ridicule of the Gospel itself, the very idea of committed faith, and the priesthood. Societal fads and diversions can make proclaiming the Gospel a mighty struggle.

And at times, "Alexander the coppersmith" walks into our lives. He, she, or they are the ones whose hot-headed complaints, unjust judgments, anonymous letters, petty gossip, or unyielding hostility smarts to the core because it is aimed deliberately and squarely at us. Whether it is a case of personality conflict, ideological difference, disagreement with decisions we have made, mental illness, our inability to meet unreasonable expectations, pure malice, or the uncomfortable fact that we may, in fact, be in the wrong, we feel Alexander's shadow. It can consume us emotionally and spiritually if we allow it.

It is not always possible to reconcile with Alexander or undo his harm, but we still must deal with our reaction to him. What does the Lord want to teach us through Alexander's looming presence?

To begin with an obvious possibility, Alexander might be right, and it is my pride that hurts. If I have done wrong, I must ask forgiveness. Perhaps God is teaching me the meaning of conversion.

If the personal injury I feel because of Alexander's actions is natural and understandable precisely because he meant to do me harm, I am called to forgive. Perhaps God is teaching me the meaning of mercy.

Alexander may have no idea he has such a hold on me. Perhaps what I am experiencing is the way he deals with all of life, the way he treats his family and coworkers, the way he conducts business in his neighborhood association. But the fact that Alexander may have little self-awareness does not make me feel any better. He still gets my dander up just by showing up. Perhaps God is teaching me the meaning of patience.

Though his methods may be annoying and unkind, perhaps Alexander represents a segment of the parish or archdiocese whose voice should be heard. In such a case he may feel like a threat but is not. Perhaps God is teaching me to listen more attentively and less defensively.

Not infrequently, even as Alexander is doing me "a great deal of harm," he might very well be the one who is hurting the most. Who knows what is going on at home or at work, what demons plague his days, what silent suffering grips him? Perhaps God is teaching me the meaning of compassion.

Alexander's behavior might indeed be rooted in malice and meanness, and the public nature of his words or actions might make it necessary to just as publicly set the record straight. Perhaps God is teaching me how to act prudently and justly but not vengefully.

No one may be aware that I have felt Alexander's venom so deeply, and the ferocity with which I clutch the offense so close to my chest might allow it to infect me more severely than I recognize. It is wise and charitable not to poison others against Alexander; but perhaps God wants me to unburden myself with a trusted friend, a spiritual director, or a confessor, and thereby heal me.

There may be nothing personal about it. Perhaps Alexander purely and simply rejects the Gospel of Jesus Christ and even feels the need to work against its proclamation. Perhaps God is asking me to trust in His plan, His truth, His wisdom, and His timing.

Sold into slavery by his brothers, Joseph's personal saga came to a dramatic climax as they came to him begging for food. When finally he revealed his identity to the very ones who had done him harm, he said: "I am your brother Joseph, whom you sold into Egypt. But now do not be distressed, and do not be angry with yourselves for having sold me here. It was really for the sake of saving lives that God sent me here ahead of you" (Gen 45:4-5). Years later, after their father Jacob's death, the brothers feared that Joseph would have a change of heart. But he reassured them: "Do not fear. Can I take the place of God? Even though you meant harm to me, God meant it for good, to achieve his present end, the survival of many people" (Gen 50:19-20).

At the conclusion of a prayer he composed on the inside cover of his breviary while imprisoned in the Tower of London, Thomas More wrote: "Give me thy grace, good Lord . . . To think my most enemies my best friends, For the brethren of Joseph could never have done him so much good with their love and favour as they did him with their malice and hatred."

When the circumstances of ministry are marked with opposition, we can be affected quite personally and painfully. But God can bring good out of every circumstance. He can deepen our faith through every trial. His plan will unfold in his time.

Many people might be surprised to learn about challenges faced by ministers of the Gospel, but Paul would not be surprised at all. The likes of Alexander, Hymenaeus, and Demas challenge us, no doubt about it. But with Paul we also know that the Lord stands by us and "will rescue us from every evil threat and will bring us safe to his heavenly kingdom" (2 Tim 4:18). Not only that: Prisca and Aquila, the family of Onesiphorus, Erastus, Trophimus, Eubulus, Pudens, Linus, and Claudia—all friends of the Lord—are with us on the way.

Sincerely in Christ,

+ Peter Sartain

Archbishop Peter Sartain

14

Grace and Class

Dear Brothers in the Lord,

I once heard a radio interview featuring several people who lived through the Great Depression. One question had to do with how neighbors helped neighbors when times were tough. A man recounted an incident when his parents, aware that a nearby family did not have enough to eat, prepared more supper than his family needed. They sent one of their kids next door with the "leftovers" and the explanation that "by mistake" too much had been prepared, and his parents wondered if they could "help make sure it didn't go to waste." The neighbors gratefully accepted, their dignity respected and embarrassment avoided.

The interview brought back memories of a skinned knee, a spilled mincemeat pie, a 100-dollar bill, and a Pinewood Derby. Through each I learned a valuable lesson about the meaning of charity and human respect.

The house in which my family lived until I was about six years old was located in a neighborhood of homes built mostly in the 1920s. My father was a pharmacist, and in those days it was common for pharmacists to be looked upon as quasi-doctors and called "Doc." Arriving home from our store one afternoon, through the chain-link fence he heard the pain-filled cries of a man who rented the ramshackle apartment above the neighbor's garage. The man had somehow been injured, and blood was streaming down his leg as he sat on the wooden steps leading up to his rooms. I watched as my father, without a moment's hesitation and still wearing his crisp white apothecary shirt, grabbed a first-aid kit and then cleaned and bandaged the bloody wound.

I couldn't have been more than five at the time, but I understood that something more than a good job of bandaging had taken place. I didn't know how the injury had been inflicted, but it seemed that the circumstances were suspicious, the kind that could have gotten the tenant in trouble with the landlord. Perhaps it was alcohol, perhaps something else, but clearly more was at stake than a bleeding knee. My father did not ask any questions but simply put his skills to work as the poor man apparently knew he would. The man's dignity had been respected and embarrassment avoided.

A few years later we moved to a new neighborhood, and at the age of eight I joined the Cub Scouts. My father's health had begun to fail, with circulation problems affecting his manual dexterity. It came time for the Pinewood Derby, a high point for eight-year-old boys, who with their dads build small cars from kits containing a block of pine, plastic wheels, and nail axles. When mom and we kids arrived home from church one Sunday, we found my dad sitting at the kitchen table, frustrated and embarrassed by his failed attempt to get a jump-start on my car. His handsaw was on the table, and he held in his lap the block of pine, now disfigured by a deep, jagged cut in just the wrong place. Sadness was written all over his face, no doubt because he could see it written on mine.

I don't know who made a phone call or who pulled some strings, but within a few days I was invited to my Den Mother's house and told to bring along my damaged block of wood. Ushered into her husband's garage workshop, I saw a grinning Mr. Bill Maier, who asked for my kit and, eyeing the splintery gash, acted as if it was the perfect beginning for the most beautiful car in the world. Grabbing a few power tools and letting me help as much as I could, within half an hour he handed me the sleekest pinewood car ever made by an eight-year-old. I proudly painted it red, connected the wheels and axles, and carefully positioned the numbered decals. I lost the Derby, but my car (which still bore more than a trace of its original wound) was nothing to laugh at. Dignity had been respected and embarrassment avoided, for both me and my dad.

Some years later my family went through a long period of financial strain caused by my father's poor health. This was not something our parents could hide from us. We knew money was tight, and like any kids our worry was accompanied by a touch of embarrassment. One day our grandmother and three aunts traveled to Memphis to have dinner with us, and for dessert mom baked a mincemeat pie. Throughout the afternoon she tried to be a good hostess and keep the mood light, though doing so was a struggle because of family concerns. When it was time for dessert, she opened the oven door to retrieve the pie, but the potholders slipped and the pie went crashing to the floor. My grandmother, my aunts, my dad, and we kids all recognized that the ruined mincemeat pie symbolized the end of mom's rope. Quietly everyone pitched in to clean up.

I don't recall who said what or how long it took, but with the help of my grandmother and aunts we made it past that painfully symbolic moment, and gradually the mood brightened. To the end of their lives, even when restricted by age and illness, my aunts had the ability to calm any situation by the sheer force of their goodness. It wasn't long after "the mincemeat pie night" that mom called us kids together to show us a 100-dollar bill sent by her sisters. I still remember her words as she held the bill: "I want you to know what your aunts have done for us." Our dignity had been respected and embarrassment avoided.

On Holy Thursday many of us priests had the privilege of washing the feet of parishioners after the example of Jesus. "I have given you a model to follow, so that as I have done for you, you should also do." Washing feet is an extraordinarily significant gesture, one that literally *puts us in our place.*

The one who washes feet not because he is coerced as a slave but because he is impelled by love sees, respects, and exalts the dignity of the ones to whom the feet belong. Clearly the apostles were caught off guard by Jesus' unanticipated footwashing, for their feet bore the embarrassing sweat, gritty dust, and filthy residue of the day. Jesus knelt down before them, making himself small once again, so they could comprehend something new about the quality of his love for them and the quality of the love they were to show others.

Meditating on Mark 10:42-45, Pope Benedict writes:

> At that moment when the Lord of the world comes and undertakes the slave's task of foot-washing—which is, in turn, only an illustration of the way he washes our feet all through our lives—we have a totally different picture. God . . . doesn't want to trample on us but kneels down before us so as to exalt us. The mystery of the greatness of God is seen precisely in the fact that he can be small. . . . Only when power is changed from the inside, . . . and we accept Jesus and his way of life, whose whole self is there in the action of foot-washing, only then can the world be healed and the people be able to live at peace with one another.[1]

I have no doubt that I would have been horribly embarrassed had I been among the group whose feet were washed by Jesus at the Last

Supper. Jesus' desire, however, was not to embarrass but to train those he was sending forth in his name. The quality of their love had to be the same as his. In fact, their love had to be the same as his.

Many years ago, my dignity and that of others was bolstered by simple acts and attitudes of humble service. A skinned knee, a Pinewood Derby, a spilled mincemeat pie, and a 100-dollar bill were occasions when I saw Jesus at work in the stuff of growing up. To be sensitively on the lookout for the troubles of others, to tend to them quietly without pointing them out or belaboring them, to share with the poor without exposing them to public scrutiny, to remove the embarrassment of others by acts of warmth and kindness, *to seek out feet to wash*—that is how we respect the God-given dignity of others. That is how we exalt them by becoming small ourselves.

Not long before she died, mom told me of her recent encounter with the priest who had been our pastor during those years of struggle. Unbeknownst to me until that day, she had sought his counsel on more than one occasion. She seized the opportunity of their chance meeting to thank him for his help those many years before. He replied, "Catherine, we had to get those kids raised, didn't we?" It was a perfect, gracious, priestly response.

In *Dives in Misericordia*, Blessed John Paul II writes about *hesed*, God's goodness, loving-kindness, and grace. He explains that even when Israel was unfaithful to God, God was faithful—true to himself—and thus revealed the "deeper aspect" of *hesed*: "love that gives, love more powerful than betrayal, grace stronger than sin" (n. 52).

We, his priests, are pitcher, basin, and towel in the hands of the Lord Jesus, whose loving-kindness flows like living water through the Church. We are true to ourselves when we allow him to use us as instruments of his Divine Mercy.

Sincerely in Christ,

+ *Peter Sartain*

Archbishop Peter Sartain

Note

1. Joseph Cardinal Ratzinger, *God and the World: Believing and Living in Our Time*, trans. Henry Taylor (San Francisco: Ignatius Press, 2002), 259–60.

15

Whose Place Is It?

Dear Brothers in the Lord,

In June 2008 I returned to Little Rock to participate in the ordination and installation of my successor, Bishop Anthony Taylor. To an extent that surprised me, I was caught off guard by the experience of watching someone "take my place." It wasn't "my" place, of course, and never had been. But having the opportunity once again to greet the priests and people of a diocese I had come to love was both joyful and bittersweet. I caught myself scanning the large congregation of more than three thousand during the ordination liturgy, recognizing faces and recalling names and details of their lives. I shook more hands than I could count and promised to pray for many.

As my mind wandered, I began to wonder: Did I handle this situation well? Was I kind to that person? Did I work as hard as I could for the good of these people? Did I offend and neglect to ask forgiveness? Did I spread the Gospel as God called me to do? Did I tend to the poor, the immigrant, the imprisoned? Did I do a good job?

Providentially for me, Bishop Taylor had chosen Luke 17:7-10 as the text for Vespers.

> Who among you would say to your servant who has just come in from plowing or tending sheep in the field, "Come here immediately and take your place at table"? Would he not rather say to him, "Prepare something for me to eat. Put on your apron and wait on me

while I eat and drink. You may eat and drink when I am finished"? Is he grateful to that servant because he did what was commanded? So should it be with you. When you have done all you have been commanded, say, "We are unprofitable servants; we have done what we were obliged to do."

Although the Lord's parable sounds harsh, we understand its meaning: that in fulfilling the tasks of discipleship, we are truly only doing our duty, for it is all God's work. In fact, everything we do is both an act of gratitude for what he has done for us and an act of cooperation with what he is doing through us.

Bishop Taylor explained how this passage is the origin of a bishop's reference to himself in the Eucharistic Prayer, "for me, your unworthy servant." The bishop, the priest, the deacon, the disciple, all do the work of the Lord, not their own work. Whatever "profit" is gained from ministry is not due to our efforts but to the grace of God.

Bishop Taylor's comments were just what I needed that night to spur me simply to thank God for the opportunity to serve the people of Arkansas and now, this diocese. But they also reminded me of you, especially those retiring or changing assignments this week. I think we almost always experience a tinge—and often more than a tinge—of sadness when we move from one parish to another or when we transition to retirement. It would be only natural that questions flow through our minds: How did I do? Could I have done more? Is God pleased? What will the next assignment be like? How will I let go of a parish I love? Will I go stir crazy in retirement?

I had the privilege of being pastor of a parish that my predecessor had served for thirty-five years. Msgr. Paul Clunan led his flock in a marvelously clear and simple manner, and as his successor I was the beneficiary of his extraordinary leadership. He never sought a niche for himself; he simply undertook the role of pastor in a uniquely loving way, confident in the wisdom of the Church that people hunger for the ordinary ministry of priests. He did not have to add meaning to the priesthood because he knew that by being a servant of God for the people they would be fed in a way quite beyond him. He concentrated on doing what pertained uniquely to his priestly vocation and enlisted the help of others to do the rest. Beyond that, he made sure that he was present in the lives of parishioners. He wouldn't have put it this way, but Msgr. Clunan understood instinctively and unself-consciously that as a priest he was an icon of Christ, and that he was not his own.

I'll never forget the day I moved in as the new pastor. Msgr. Clunan was waiting for me upstairs in my new quarters in the rectory, sitting alone in his easy chair, no doubt reflecting somewhat sadly on the thirty-five years that were coming to an end. That day he handed over the people of the parish to me, he let go of an operation he had refined into a well-tuned instrument, and he moved on. Hearing me climb the stairs, he stood up, extended his hand in a warm handshake, and said, "Pete, I love these people, and I know you will, too. You'll do a good job." That day I learned in a new way the meaning of *kenosis*.

Blessed John Paul II writes in "Radiation of Fatherhood":

> I have decided to eliminate from my vocabulary the word "my." How can I use that word when I know that everything is Yours? Even if it isn't You who give birth every time a human person is born, the one giving birth belongs to You. I myself am more "Yours" than "mine." So I have learned that I may not say "mine" of that which is Yours. I may not say, think or feel it. I must free myself, empty myself of this—I must possess nothing, I must not wish to possess anything (here "my" means "my own").[1]

The Holy Father's words are a striking reminder to us priests that even the people we serve are not "mine" or "ours." They are his, purchased at a great price, entrusted to us to shepherd and love, to guide and protect, to offer back to him as a holy gift. Only the one who learns to let go of the word "my" can give himself without counting the cost. Blessed John Paul was referring to a certain kind of *kenosis*. To recognize that even our words are not our own, that they have a power beyond us, that in fact nothing of our ministry is truly "ours," requires an emptying of our egos in order to allow God's words to echo through all we say and do.

But handing over the power to God does something else as well—it frees us of the anxiety of having to be successful, fix every problem and tend to every need. It allows us to let go when we've finished the homily that was not as eloquent as we had hoped, to move on when the assignment is ended, and to fall asleep when night comes and it is time to get some rest.

In *Paths to Interior Silence*, Edith Stein writes:

> God is there in these moments of rest and can give us in a single instant exactly what we need. Then the rest of the day can take its course, under the same effort and strain, perhaps, but in peace. And

when night comes, and you look back over the day and see how much you planned that has gone undone, and all the reasons you have to be embarrassed and ashamed: just take everything exactly as it is, put it in God's hands and leave it with him. Then you will be able to rest in him—really rest—and start the next day as a new life.

Saint Maximilian Kolbe offered his life in substitution for a fellow prisoner of the concentration camp at Auschwitz, a young husband and father who was about to be executed in retribution for the attempted escape of another prisoner. André Frossard titled his biography of Kolbe *Forget Not Love: The Passion of Maximilian Kolbe,* after a beautiful incident toward the end of his life.[2] In the weeks following Hitler's invasion of Poland in September 1939, Kolbe had been ordered to close his monastery of over six hundred friars. As he bade farewell he gave last-minute instructions, practical advice for what was to come, spiritual advice to maintain their vocations under harsh circumstances, and fatherly advice to keep up their spirits. And from the doorstep he gave them one last bit of advice: "Do not forget love." "Do not forget love," he said, as his brothers left the monastery for an uncertain future.

Do not forget love! If we pray, our love will grow. If we celebrate the sacraments with devotion, our love will grow. If we put others first, our love will grow. If we forgive, our love will grow. If we live simply, our love will grow. If we learn to give ourselves in sacrifice, bitterness will flee and love will grow. If we listen to our people, our love will grow. If we keep our hearts open to their suffering and their yearning, our love will grow. If we hold fast to the Lord Jesus, our love will grow. If we love, our love will grow. Do not forget love!

I could easily make a list of the many things I have left undone in Tennessee, Arkansas, Illinois, and Washington. Sometimes I think about them, but the Lord reminds me to let go. Though we move or retire, the Lord remains and abides steadfastly, loving his people with his own heart and through the hearts, words, and deeds of those who come after us. He asked us to be his servants at a certain time and place, and he made use of us beyond our capacity to recognize just how. Because he is at work, we can move on in peace. The good news is that we can move on in peace not just when our assignment changes, or when it's time to retire; we can move forward in peace every day. We are unprofitable servants, instruments of God whose power to love, heal, forgive, reconcile, and nourish is greater than we could possibly imagine.

After we have done all we have been called to do, and after we have loved the flock entrusted to our care, we will not have come close to exhausting the spring of life flowing from the side of Christ through the Church. One cannot exhaust the inexhaustible. The reason we undertake all that we undertake is this: we are filled with hope in Christ.

Sincerely in Christ,

+ *Peter Sartain*

Archbishop Peter Sartain

Notes

1. John Paul II, qtd. in *Rise, Let Us Be On Our Way* (New York: Warner Books, 2004), 135.

2. Andre Frossard, *Forget Not Love: The Passion of Maximilian Kolbe* (San Francisco: Ignatius Press, 1991).

16

Loving Difficult People

Dear Brothers in the Lord,

A pastor once asked to meet to discuss his difficult parish assignment. British by birth, he had a particularly delightful way of expressing himself. He exploded with adjectives as he assessed the state of the parish:

> My Lord, they are obstreperous, mulish, conniving, scheming, defiant, and fussy. They construct road blocks at every turn, they are not open to new ideas, they are cliquish and intolerant. They would object if the Lord Himself were their pastor. They treat me as if I were only the latest ox in a team bought to plow their fields. They keep a record of the length of my homilies and insist on the subjects about which I should preach. I cannot walk across the parking lot after Mass without one of them telling me what I ought do or not do. They thrive on rumor and pry into one another's lives as if nothing else in the world matters to them.

Pausing for a moment, he added, with a smile I will never forget, "And I love them!"

He did love them, and after a while, they loved him. In fact, it was precisely because of his love that the parish changed, and for the better.

We will not always like those to whom God sends us, and they will not always like us. At times that will be the case because of their behavior or their history, at times because of ours. We can tolerate, ignore, or try to escape such a situation—and live in unreality. Or we can love the unlikeable—acknowledging that God has sent us to them, that each of them is beloved to him, that Jesus himself is within them.

Giving a retreat to a group of Missionaries of Charity many years ago, I wondered out loud in one my talks whether the sisters ever felt repulsed by those they served, whether they found it hard to bandage the wounds, change the sheets, put up with the harsh words, and deal with the bizarre behavior of some of their poor. As I looked around the room, I saw heads nodding softly in agreement. We often enter situations that are unpleasant and conflicted. What are we to bring to such settings?

Five Loaves and Two Fish is Cardinal Francis-Xavier van Thuan's spiritual memoir of imprisonment under the North Vietnamese. Because his appointment as Coadjutor Archbishop of Saigon in 1975 did not meet the approval of communist authorities, he was placed under house arrest. Seven months later, he was formally arrested and spent almost ten years in a variety of prisons and reeducation camps, often in solitary confinement. He recounts this fascinating and powerful incident:

> One night when I was sick, in the prison of Phú Khánh, I saw a policeman walk by and I shouted: "For goodness' sake, I am very sick; please give me some medicine!" He responded: "There is no goodness here, nor love; there is only responsibility."[1]

The policeman had made his perspective clear: the sole arbiter of his actions was responsibility. Reflecting on the tense atmosphere of his relationship with the guards, the cardinal pondered his response. He writes:

> One night, a thought came to me: "Francis, you are still very rich. You have the love of Christ in your heart. Love them as Jesus has loved you." The next day I began to love them, *to love Jesus in them*, smiling, exchanging kind words.[2]

He soon began to notice that the tense atmosphere changed dramatically for the better.

Retired Vice Admiral Edward W. Cooke is a close friend whom I hold in the highest regard. Now in his late 80s, his life has been a succession of distinguished careers—Navy, business, and Church. While reading Cardinal van Thuan's book, I called Ed to discuss a conversation we had more than ten years earlier. I had asked him what single word he would use to describe the driving force behind each of the careers he had chosen. He thought for a moment and said, "For the Navy, it was 'duty.' For business, 'expedience.' For the Church, 'hope.'" I think Cardinal van Thuan would have agreed.

Whether we recognize it or not, each of us allows some driving force to arbitrate our attitudes, words, and decisions. It is the perspective out of which we live, out of which our sense of well-being and fulfillment is ultimately determined. The distinguishing mark of Christian faith is that it offers the only driving force, the only arbiter, which integrates and fulfills all others: hope in Christ and his abiding love. The cardinal had been schooled in Christian love since childhood, but consciously deciding to make it the driving force beneath the tension-filled life of deprivation he experienced in prison, he discovered its power. In the most dramatic days of imprisonment, unable to pray and on the brink of exhaustion, he would repeat to himself: "I am the living testament of the love of Jesus." Not only did his life begin to change; the lives of those around him changed. His love became a lure, a net, to bring them close, even unwittingly, to the love of Christ.

Saint John of the Cross writes: "Where there is no love, put love, and you will draw out love."[3] We will inevitably find ourselves in pastoral situations where love has been smothered or seemingly snuffed out. Such situations can bring out the worst in us and others, and the ugliness may seem impenetrable. We will be tempted to speak ill of others. Those to whom we are sent may be in fact unlikeable in such situations, but they are never unlovable. It is precisely *to love them* that we have been sent. To love them, to love Jesus in them, to put love where there is no love—means hoping in the Lord. The cardinal could have been nice to his captors as a means to an end or out of determined obedience to Jesus' admonition to turn the other cheek. He chose instead to be a living testament of the love of Jesus, and through him they encountered Jesus.

It takes great courage and humility to offer oneself as a living testament. The way of the Lord is not expedient, and the conventional wisdom of our corner of the world may consider his way foolish or naive. Anyone engaged in the service of the Lord, however, is engaged in a lifelong process of conversion. The one on the road of conversion realizes that it is always too early to give up. As St. John Climacus writes in his *Ladder of Divine Ascent*: "Repentance is the renewal of baptism and a contract with God for a fresh start in life . . . [It] is the daughter of hope and the refusal to despair."[4]

Our conversion will be authentic, and our reflection of Christ clear, only if we pray. To undertake priestly ministry without praying is sheer foolishness. It is prayer that integrates the varied aspects of our lives, prayer that draws us closer to the heart of God, prayer that chisels and refines us (for all of us need both chiseling and delicate refinement) into images of Christ, prayer that strengthens our hope, prayer that ensures we are following Christ and not our own agenda, prayer that sustains us when we find ourselves in difficult pastoral situations, prayer that teaches us to love the unlikeable.

As Pope Benedict writes in *Spe salvi:*

> When no one listens to me any more, God still listens to me. When I can no longer talk to anyone or call upon anyone, I can always talk to God. When there is no longer anyone to help me deal with a need or expectation that goes beyond the human capacity for hope, he can help me. When I have been plunged into complete solitude; if I pray I am never totally alone. (32)
>
> When we pray properly we undergo a process of inner purification which opens us up to God and thus to our fellow human beings as well. In prayer we must learn what we can truly ask of God—what is worthy of God. . . . We must learn to purify our desires and our hopes. We must free ourselves from the hidden lies with which we deceive ourselves. God sees through them, and when we come before God, we too are forced to recognize them. (33)

To pray is to breathe in the atmosphere of repentance, conversion, and the mercy of Jesus; to pray is to begin to let go of desires that are not of God; to pray is to hope in God, to hand over everything to God. The process of inner purification to which we are called in prayer, the purification which cleanses us of discouragement, bitterness, and self-centeredness, also opens us up to our fellow human beings *precisely because it opens us to God.* In other words, our personal prayer is "for us," but it is also "for others," because it enlarges our capacity for hope and love and reorients us through God to all those he loves.

One of the revered priests of the Diocese of Memphis would never say a harsh word about another person. He surely had reason to be perturbed and aggravated from time to time, but the most critical comment he would allow himself to make about another was, "I think he's a little nervous." He did not excuse bad behavior. He forgave it, because he loved his parishioners with the love of Jesus.

Sincerely in Christ,

+ *Peter Sartain*

Archbishop Peter Sartain

Notes

1. Archbishop François-Xavier Nguyen van Thuan, *Five Loaves and Two Fish* (Washington, DC: Morley Books, 2000), 53.

2. Ibid., 54.

3. John of the Cross, Letter 26, in *The Collected Works of St. John of the Cross*, rev. ed., trans. Kieran Kavanaugh and Otilio Rodriguez (Washington, DC: ICS Publications, 1991), 760.

4. John Climacus, "On Penitence," in *Ladder of Divine Ascent,* translated by Colm Luibheid and Norman Russell, Classics of Western Spirituality (Mahwah, NJ: Paulist Press, 1982), 121.

17

Run from Discouragement

Dear Brothers in the Lord,

Evening prayer of Monday in Week III of Ordinary Time has special meaning for me. One night not long after ordination to the priesthood, I found myself filled with anxiety and discouragement. It was a strange place to be so soon and so painfully, and there was no rational explanation for the onset of such turmoil. Armed with my breviary, I went to church and poured out my heart to the Lord. Then I began the Evening Prayer of Monday in Week III.

The brief scripture passage before the second psalm leapt off the page and began to turn things around for me: "the Lord said to Paul: Do not be afraid . . . for I am with you" (Acts 18:9).

In a way I had not experienced before, I read that verse as directed squarely at me, at that moment, in that church. And I believe the Lord used that night of frightening discouragement to begin giving me insight into a dynamic that can hinder spiritual growth, particularly for us who are given to the Lord. He began to teach me that discouragement is a clever tool of the evil one.

There are times in the life of every priest when we come face-to-face with our human frailty, our incapacity to act as we ought, our incompleteness, our inadequacy, our failure to meet both our own expectations and those of others, our lack of understanding, our infidelity to Christ, our fatigue, our hurt, our anger, our lack of progress, our inability to pray as we would like, the superficiality of our faith—and that's just the tip of the iceberg!

Every priest also confronts disappointments caused by others or by the world itself (*they* failed to act as they ought, *they* did not meet our expectations, etc.). Life as it is can be frustrating, and, as hard as we try, we are incapable of changing others or the circumstances around us. Why aren't things different? we might ask ourselves.

Needless to say, each of the situations I have mentioned can in itself be an obstacle to anyone trying to be a good disciple of the Lord. However, it is good to recognize that it is the *discouragement* that such situations drum up that can be the greatest obstacle of all. We should always be suspicious of discouragement.

When I am discouraged by failure—mine or someone else's—and allow it to paralyze or tempt me to give up, I am unwittingly assuming that I am something other than I am. Though it does not seem so, when I let discouragement overtake me, I am assuming that I ought to be able to do everything on my own, that I ought to be able to fix myself, that failure should never happen if I am serious about being a priest, that I ought to be able to do everything without anyone's help and even (here is the most dangerous part) without God's help. I mention that we hold these assumptions unwittingly, and it takes a few moments of prayerful reflection to recognize them for what they are: the shrewd incursion of the devil into the desires of our hearts.

The onset of discouragement is a prime opportunity to understand God's grace. It is not in our nature to be self-sufficient—we are whole only when we allow God to work within us. Just as we did not create ourselves, we cannot re-create ourselves, forgive our own sin, or repair ourselves. That is God's work, and he is more than eager to provide everything we need (and more), including the grace to lean unto him when we confront our frailty and the brokenness of the world.

The Prodigal Son, smarting from the abject failure of his plans, had feared that his father would not receive him back, but the father had not forgotten—and could never forget—his runaway son. His heart ached so much for the one who was lost, to whom he had given the shirt off his back (and would again, gladly), that from his front porch he strained his eyes scanning the hills to see if there was any sign of his lost one.

When finally he caught sight of the runaway he took to his heels, running toward his son to embrace him and escort him home. Here was no ordinary father; here was a father who always gave everything to his beloved sons with lavish generosity.

It is in light of this truth about our heavenly Father that we can look at ourselves. We live in the household of a Father who lavishes upon us everything we need. The parable of the Prodigal Son is not just about those individual times we sin and turn back; it is actually about the whole of our lives, for every one of us at every moment is on a rambling path toward God. What Jesus wants us to remember is that his Father is watching for us, scanning the hills to see if we show any signs of looking his direction, hoping we will slow down long enough to hear him beckoning us home to an extravagant banquet. We'll bring our blemishes and blights, our fractures and scars, our fears and discouragements. He'll clothe us in glory. It will be pretty embarrassing. And wonderful.

Discouragement is a form of alienation—from God, from the truth, from our goals, from our self-confidence, from ourselves. Often it is rooted in forgetfulness of the truths about God and his relationship with us, truths such as those revealed in the parables. The Prodigal Son had lost sight of the lifelong prodigality of his father, and I have a feeling that had the parable continued, we would have learned that once safely home he never allowed the words of his father to wander far from his consciousness: "you are here with me always; everything I have is yours" (Luke 15:31).

In times of discouragement, I find it helpful to rekindle my awareness of God's promises, the truth that endures through every situation life sends my way.

> Trust in the LORD with all your heart,
>   on your own intelligence do not rely;
> In all your ways be mindful of him,
>   and he will make straight your paths. (Prov 3:5-6)

> O Most High, when I am afraid,
>   in you I place my trust. . . .

> My wanderings you have noted;
>   are my tears not stored in your flask,
>   recorded in your book? . . .
> This I know: God is on my side. . . .
> In God I trust, I do not fear.
>   What can man do to me? (Ps 56:3-4; 9-10, 12)

> For I am convinced that neither death, nor life, nor angels, nor principalities, nor present things, nor future things, nor powers, nor height, nor depth, nor any other creature will be able to separate us from the love of God in Christ Jesus our Lord. (Rom 8:38-39)

I have told you this so that you might have peace in me. In the world you will have trouble, but take courage, I have conquered the world. (John 16:33)

"My grace is sufficient for you, for power is made perfect in weakness." (2 Cor 12:9).

"I command you: be strong and steadfast! Do not fear nor be dismayed, for the LORD, your God, is with you wherever you go." (Josh 1:9)

One night in a vision the Lord said to Paul, "Do not be afraid. Go on speaking, and do not be silent, for I am with you. No one will attack and harm you, for I have many people in this city." (Acts 18:9-10)

Jesus said to him, "I am the way and the truth and the life." (John 14:6)

Commenting on the words of Jesus, St. Thomas Aquinas encourages us to stay always on the way of Jesus, even if we are tempted for whatever reason to abandon his way:

"If, then, you are looking for the way by which you should go, take Christ, because he himself is the way. . . . It is better to limp along the way than stride along off the way. For a man who limps along the way, even if he only makes slow progress, comes to the end of the way; but one who is off the way, the more quickly he runs, the further away is he from his goal.

"If you are looking for a goal, hold fast to Christ, because he himself is the truth, where we desire to be. . . . If you are looking for a resting place, hold fast to Christ, because he himself is the life.

"Therefore hold fast to Christ if you wish to be safe. You will not be able to go astray, because he is the way. He who remains with him does not wander in trackless places; he is on the right way. Moreover he cannot be deceived, because he is the truth."[1]

Perhaps we want to run when we should walk. Perhaps we jump off the way because we think we know a better way or a shortcut. Perhaps we allow the public embarrassment of our limping to stop us in our tracks. Perhaps we are burdened by the consequences of our words or actions. Perhaps we are tempted to give up, to give in, because the obstacles seem insurmountable and the way murky and contorted. Perhaps fatigue makes us think we cannot take another step.

Discouragement is natural at certain points in our lives—but it is also unhelpful, unnecessary, and hazardous. It is one of Satan's tricks to trip us off the way. He would have us forget the truths on which we have staked our very lives. He would have us forget that God loves us. But we will not forget! God loves the limping, the frail, the fractured, the lost and the discouraged who own up to their disfigurements, their weariness, and their confusion, because in them he has vessels receptive to his grace.

It is helpful to remind ourselves that in the grace of Holy Orders God gave us what we will need for every situation to come our way. On our day of ordination, we could not possibly have foreseen the situations we would face or what would befall us as the years would go by—but God knew. He gave us what we need and in such measure that it will never be exhausted. As Paul encouraged Timothy:

> I remind you to stir into flame the gift of God that you have through the imposition of my hands. For God did not give us a spirit of cowardice but rather of power and love and self-control. So do not be ashamed of your testimony to our Lord, nor of me, a prisoner for his sake; but bear your share of hardship for the gospel with the strength that comes from God. (2 Tim 1:6-8)

My brothers in the Lord, run from discouragement and hope in God. He never takes his eyes off you, he knows what he is about in you, and he will give you what you need today.

Sincerely in Christ,

+ *Peter Sartain*

Archbishop Peter Sartain

Note

1. Thomas Aquinas, *The Exposition on John*, chap. 14, lect. 2, qtd. in the Office of Readings, *The Liturgy of the Hours*, vol. III, translated by the International Commission on English in the Liturgy (New York: Catholic Book Publishing, 1975), 315–16.

18

Surviving Gossip

Dear Brothers in the Lord,

I don't imagine it was easy for the Lord to listen to the murmuring, grumbling, and rumors that often had him as their subject. Knowing well that gossip abounded, he even asked the Twelve, "Who do people say that I am?"

How did Jesus react when the things people said about him were laced with innuendo, falsehood, and judgment? No doubt his ability to discern hearts gave him insight into their motives, but he must have been distressed by the damage done by sharp and ungoverned tongues. He wept at the thought that Jerusalem had rejected him, perhaps in part because people had been lured away by tantalizing and mean-spirited lies. He acknowledged that the prophets had known the same behind-the-scenes whispers, the same stinging ill will and mindless speculation, the same rejection.

We know it, too. But who doesn't? No one is immune from rumor (by its nature rumor is indiscriminate), and yet none of us enjoys being its subject. Rumor makes one the object of another's fascination and entertainment, grist for the mill of judgment. Rumor seems to steal something from us (our good name, our ability to explain and justify, our dignity), and the very fact that it objectifies us takes the wind out of our sails, angers and hurts us.

There's certainly nothing new under the sun. Gossip has been around since the beginning of speech, but the internet has ratcheted it up to an obsession. Television news is often mere gossip, speculation about what might happen or conjecture about a decision someone might make, accompanied by theorization about possible motives and consequences. Gossip steals headlines, but it is not news. By being spoken it has done its damage.

As pastor I often joked that the school parking lot was an occasion of sin because of the gossip that breezed from waiting car to waiting car; but the internet has trumped the parking lot. There are undeniable benefits to the internet, and I use it daily. However, websites, social networks, blogs, and texts offer a ready forum to justify, celebrate, and accelerate gossip. One can say what he wants, suggest what she wills, spread false information, categorize and condemn as they see fit. In seconds. With a worldwide audience. With no capacity to retrieve even one unfair word. These forums are all the more exasperating because of their anonymity.

Everyone is prey to rumor and gossip, including priests. What do we do with our reaction to it?

In his biography of St. John Vianney, François Trochu recounts a period when brother priests were murmuring about John, going so far as to take their gossip to the bishop. Asked why he didn't vigorously defend himself, Vianney responded with a story from his bedside companion, *The Lives of the Saints.*

> A certain saint once commanded one of his religious: "Go to the cemetery and speak as much evil of the dead as you can." The religious obeyed. Upon his return, the saint asked him, "What did they answer?" "Nothing." "Well, go back now and pay them a great many compliments." The religious obeyed once more and returned to his superior. "Surely this time they said something by way of reply." "Again nothing." "Very well," said the saint, "if people rebuke you, if they praise you, do as the dead."[1]

Vianney wrote of personal experience in one of his catechisms:

> Today I had two letters. . . . In one I am told that I am a saint, in the other that I am nothing more than a quack. The first letter gave me nothing, the second took nothing from me.[2]

When we are the subject of gossip, it is good to take stock of its effect on us. If we go to great lengths to read or investigate it with exacting precision, we run the risk of letting it ensnare us. If we let it cheat us of peace, we have traded something precious for a puff of air. If we allow ourselves to be driven to distraction over it, our energy is sapped and we risk ignoring the suffering person at our side who seeks the Lord's consolation and a word of hope.

As hard as it is to carry out this advice in practice, I find that the more quickly we dismiss rumors from our minds, the better. Handing them to the Lord for his inspection, his assessment, and his use for our good, we in effect say, "Lord, if there is something to be learned in that vicious gossip, let me learn it. If there is something in that rumor that I need to know, let me retain it but without rancor or nosiness. If I rely too much on human respect, teach me humility. When I gossip, stop me in my tracks lest I hurt someone as I have been hurt."

Many years ago, at a time I was licking my wounds after someone had deliberately prejudiced staff members against me, I came across a prayer which has helped me immensely.

> I have been misjudged and deeply offended, dear Lord, and it is hard to suppress my wounded feelings. But when I reflect on the injuries You have patiently suffered for my sake and now ask me to bear You company, I am strengthened to accept the trial for love of You in return. Let me never fear that You will ask too much of me. Of course You often ask for something that my nature rebels against, but the pain of giving it lasts only a short time, while the reward is eternal. St. Ignatius tells us to "labor to make ourselves indifferent," not necessarily "be indifferent," because we do not become indifferent or lose our sensitivities overnight. I ask for the grace to profit from this experience and, in spite of my emotions, offer the sacrifice of my will to Your divine will. Amen.[3]

Whether conveyed by word of mouth, newspaper, television, or internet, gossip and innuendo hurt. But as in all things offered to and with the Lord, even false and hurtful words can be used by him for our good. What was thoughtless or intended as spiteful becomes a blessing.

"Do not care much about who is with you and who is against you; but make it your greatest care that God is with you in everything you do."[4]

Sincerely in Christ,

+ Peter Sartain

Archbishop Peter Sartain

Notes

1. Abbé François Trochu, *The Curé D'Ars, St. Jean-Marie-Baptiste Vianney* (Charlotte: TAN Books, 1977), 293–94.

2. Ibid., 294.

3. John A. Hardon, SJ, *Fr. Hardon's Catholic Prayer Book with Meditations* (Bardstown, KY: Eternal Life, 1999), 270–71.

4. Thomas à Kempis, *The Imitation of Christ*, II.2.

19
Advent Loneliness

Dear Brothers in the Lord,

One of my closest friends, Robert, told me one Advent that he feels lonely during the holidays. His admission surprised me, because he was a doctor with a loving wife and six terrific kids, a busy practice, and many friends. Here was a man admired by his peers and sought out for advice, a man whose calendar was jammed with human interaction—but who admitted feeling lonely.

He explained that his loneliness was no one's fault and certainly not that of his family, who surrounded him with love and attention. Neither was it the fault of his coworkers, who understood the kind of care he wanted to give patients and cooperated in every way. His holiday loneliness had been part of his life for years, but he could never quite get hold of it—it remained a mystery to him even the day he told me of it.

Part of my surprise at hearing him speak of loneliness was that I knew from experience what he was talking about, but I never would have suspected he shared the experience. As pastor of a large parish with a grade school, I was surrounded by the joyous signs of Advent and Christmas. With family and friends all over town, I had an open invitation to any number of supper tables (one of my brothers-in-law says I can find my way to his kitchen table from anywhere in the world). My calendar, too, was packed with people. And yet I could say that at the holidays I sometimes feel lonely.

A few months after Robert's wife died after a brave eighteen-month battle with ovarian cancer, he traveled to Seattle to visit me for a few days, and one evening I asked if he remembered that conversation of long ago. "I remember it well," he said. Thinking about that conversation further, he said, "Pete, it's the *longing*. It's the longing for where we're headed."

Many people are lonely, and for a variety of reasons. *Being* alone is not necessarily a cause of loneliness, but needless to say, it can be. Ironically, the solitude that makes one person lonely might be the very thing another person actively seeks. We can feel lonely because we are far from home, because a loved one has died, because no one seems to understand our plight, because of nostalgia for the past, because we miss our former parish, because we are afraid to confide in someone about a struggle that preoccupies us, because we face a decision about which no one else is aware, because illness has separated us from our routine, because we are estranged from those who matter most to us, because of depression, because of sin, because of. . . . The list goes on.

Another of the ironies of loneliness is that it can make us narcissistic: *feeling* alone I begin to assess the people and conditions around me in terms of their treatment of *me,* and that self-centeredness can cause my loneliness to deepen. We also have to be alert to the traps that lay ready to ensnare us when we feel lonely—overindulgence in food or drink, temptations of the flesh, bitterness, and even the misuse of authority or other passive-aggressive means of asserting ourselves (as if to say, back-handedly, "Don't forget me! I am here!").

An obvious antidote to loneliness is to take initiative in reaching out to someone else—call a relative, friend, or spiritual director; write a note; take a walk across the parish campus and visit with parishioners. Still, there is an indefinable, elusive quality to loneliness that can weigh us down precisely because we cannot figure it out or fix it. It is that quality that I believe is fertile ground for a priest's Advent. It need not be a burden. Given the proper perspective, we can view it as a good thing. Perhaps a certain measure of loneliness is even necessary for us priests.

I wonder if rather than spending time trying to repair our loneliness, we would be better served by allowing it to teach us. Although it is not possible to dissect loneliness in order to fix it, there are three aspects of its elusiveness which I find helpful to examine at Advent: incompletion, longing, and expectation. The three are closely joined.

I often notice with frustration that my thoughts and behavior fall short of the example Christ offers me, the ideal for which I long. He is everything to me, and yet I do not always live as if he is everything to me. My response to him is at times halfhearted and incomplete, and I long to be more generous of heart. There lies at my core a profound incompletion, a constitutional loneliness, which I am utterly unable to resolve. I have come to see it as a good thing, as a sign and invitation: it constantly reminds me of my total emptiness before God. My sense of incompletion and loneliness does not represent some kind of gap (as if to say, "If only for that gap, that hole, I would be fine"). It is in fact an inkling of something profoundly true about me: I am an entirely empty vessel that will not be filled with any measure of human relationship or created thing. Only God can fill me, and once I allow him to fill me every other element of my life falls into its proper place.

Saint Augustine suggests that this sense of incompletion and desire is God's way of stretching us for something greater. Commenting on 1 John, he writes:

> The entire life of a good Christian is in fact an exercise of holy desire. You do not yet see what you long for, but the very act of desiring prepares you, so that when he comes you may see and be utterly satisfied.

> Suppose you are going to fill some holder or container, and you know you will be given a large amount. Then you set about stretching your sack or wineskin or whatever it is. Why? Because you know the quantity you will have to put in it and your eyes tell you there is not enough room. By stretching it, therefore, you increase the capacity of the sack, and this is how God deals with us. Simply by making us wait he increases our desire, which in turn enlarges the capacity of our soul, making it able to receive what is to be given to us.[1]

There is no doubt that the sense of incompletion can cause us to be discouraged to the point of giving up. But Augustine says God uses our waiting to stretch and increase the capacity of our soul. He wants us to be ready for what he intends to give us, as well as its quantity, and capable of the manner in which he will fulfill our expectations.

Expanding on Augustine's image of stretching, perhaps we can uncover still other hidden graces in loneliness. Recognizing our incompletion, admitting our utter emptiness, and longing for the fulfillment of God's promises, we see how:

1. **God stretches us** *forward.* The prophets proclaimed the presence
   and promises of God and in so doing stretched the people of Israel
   forward in expectation of God. Leaning into their future with God,
   they lived in expectation; and leaning, stretching, and longing to
   see him, they were gradually being made more capable of receiving
   him. God was literally making room in them for his Advent. This
   same stretching forward appears in Paul's letter to the Romans:

   > . . . you know the time; it is the hour now for you to awake from
   > sleep. For our salvation is nearer now than when we first believed;
   > the night is advanced, the day is at hand. Let us then throw off the
   > works of darkness [and] put on the armor of light; let us conduct
   > ourselves properly as in the day. (Rom 13:11-12)

2. **God stretches us** *outward.* When we experience loneliness, God
   places us in solidarity with his beloved poor: those who hunger and
   thirst, who have no place to live, who have been abandoned by
   family and friends, who are in prison and sick and literally alone.
   It is vital for our spiritual lives that we cultivate solidarity with
   them, because Jesus was anointed "to bring glad tidings to the poor"
   (Luke 4:18) and was born into poverty himself. *Spiritually, he wants
   us to be poor in spirit so that we will listen hungrily to the Gospel.* Minis-
   terially, he wants us to be compassionate in word and deed. Loneliness can make us focus exclusively on ourselves, but God desires
   to use it to stretch us outwardly and make us one with the poor, for
   Jesus was one of them.

3. **God stretches us** *inward.* The great invitation of the spiritual life is
   depth—to allow God into the depths of my life, to give myself from
   the depths of my soul. The temptation to live on the surface is great,
   and it is easy to be bounced around like a pinball by the meetings
   and events on our daily schedule. Living from the depths brings
   balance and peace to a hectic life, and prayer is the way to the
   depths. Ironically, when we pray we may rarely be aware that we
   are reaching our depths, but we are—and allowing God to stretch
   us inwardly, we sink roots and foundation in him. He is our anchor
   in wind and wave.

Saint Thomas Aquinas writes that "prayer is the spokesman of hope."[2]
Perhaps what we experience most often is the longing to pray more or
better, and we should recognize that our longing is already prayer be-

cause it emerges spontaneously and unfiltered from our depths. In many ways, it is our deepest self telling us to seek God, to hope in God. In his commentary on Psalm 37:9-10 (38:9-10), Augustine gives further insight into such longing:

> "*All my desire is before you, Lord.* Not before human beings, who cannot see my heart, but before you is all my desire." Let your desire too be before him, and there your Father, who sees in secret, will reward you (Matt 6:6). This very desire is your prayer, and if your desire is continuous, your prayer is continuous too. The apostle meant what he said, *Pray without ceasing* (1 Thes 5:17) . . .
>
> Whatever else you may be engaged upon, if you are all the while desiring that Sabbath [that kingdom of God which flesh and blood will not possess], you never cease to pray. If you do not want to interrupt your prayer, let your desire be uninterrupted.[3]

Better yet, as St. Paul writes, "In the same way, the Spirit too comes to the aid of weakness; for we do not know how to pray as we ought, but the Spirit itself intercedes with inexpressible groanings" (Rom 8:26).

God also stretches us inwardly because he wants to fill us with mercy, and sorrow for sin is our response to that stretching. Augustine continues his commentary on 1 John:

> Let me return to the example I have already used, of filling an empty container. God means to fill each of you with what is good, so cast out what is bad! If he wishes to fill you with honey and you are full of sour wine, where is the honey to go? The vessel must be emptied of its contents and then be cleansed. Yes, it must be cleansed even if we have to work hard and scour it. It must be made fit for the new thing, whatever it may be.[4]

God does not want us to get stuck in sorrow and shame, but he can use them to purify us and stretch our capacity to receive his mercy and any other "new thing" he desires to give us.

German Jesuit Alfred Delp was an outspoken critic of the Third Reich and a participant in the German Resistance. Known as a dynamic and insightful preacher, he was imprisoned in 1944 and martyred by the Nazis a year later. Delp wrote meditations (usually while handcuffed) on small scraps of paper during solitary confinement in Berlin's Tegel Prison. A favorite theme was Advent. In a meditation for the First Sunday of Advent, 1944, Delp suggests that the basic condition of life always has an Advent dimension: boundaries, and hunger, and thirst, and lack of fulfillment, and promise, and movement toward one another. That means, however, that we basically remain without shelter, under way, and open until the final encounter, with all the humble blessedness and painful pleasure of this openness.

Therefore there is no interim finality, and the attempt to create final conclusions is an old temptation of mankind. Hunger and thirst, and desert journeying, and the survival teamwork of mountaineers on a rope—these are the truth of our human condition. . . .

May God help us to wake up to ourselves and in doing so, to move from ourselves toward Him.

"Universi, qui te exspectant, non confundentur" [Those who wait for You will not be disappointed]. May we know and acknowledge the hunger and thirst above and beyond ourselves. Indeed, this is no waiting without hope. Rather, the heart receives the delightful warmth known to those who wait with the certitude that the other is coming and has already set out on the way.[5]

Perhaps what we sometimes identify as loneliness is not loneliness at all but our souls crying out to God in spontaneous response to his longing for us, reminding us that we will never be satisfied until we see him face-to-face.

As the deer longs for streams of water,
    so my soul longs for you, O God.
My soul thirsts for God, the living God.
    When can I enter and see the face of God? (Ps 42:1-2)

All of this longing and desire, this stretching and expectation of God's fullness, this loneliness and emptiness, have *caritas* as their ultimate end: for that with which God fills us is to be given away. Did not Christ come to us in order to *give himself*? Father Robert Barron writes:

God's life is had, as it were, on the fly: when one receives it as a gift, he must give it away, since it only exists in gift form, and when he gives it away he will find more of it flooding into his heart.[6]

Or, as I once heard Francis Cardinal George phrase it in a homily, "The only thing we will take with us to heaven is what we have given away."

There is probably no better way to prepare for Christmas than to follow our longing and loneliness, admit our emptiness and weakness, and acknowledge our incapacity to save ourselves. To admit the depth of our need is not reason for shame—it is a sign of expectation and welcome to the Savior, the Father's response to our longing. May he stretch us more and more this Advent, that we may be even more capable of receiving him and have even more to give away at Christmas.

Sincerely in Christ,

+ *Peter Sartain*

Archbishop Peter Sartain

Notes

1. Augustine, *Tractates on the First Letter of Saint John*, qtd. in the Office of Readings, *The Liturgy of the Hours*, vol. III, trans. the International Commission on English in the Liturgy (New York: Catholic Book Publishing, 1975), 220.

2. Qtd. in Christoph Cardinal Schönborn, OP, *Loving the Church* (San Francisco: Ignatius Press, 1998), 156.

3. Augustine, *Expositions of the Psalms 33–50*, trans. Maria Boulding, OSB, The Works of Saint Augustine: A Translation for the 21st Century III/16 (Hyde Park, NY: New City Press, 2000), 156–57.

4. Augustine, qtd. in the Office of Readings, *The Liturgy of the Hours*, vol. III, 221.

5. Alfred Delp, *Advent of the Heart: Seasonal Sermons and Prison Writings 1941–1944* (San Francisco: Ignatius Press, 2006), 51–52.

6. Robert Barron, *Catholicism: A Journey to the Heart of the Faith* (New York: Image Books, 2011), 41.

20

Christmas Freedom

" 'The holy one, the true,
    who holds the key of David,
    who opens and no one shall close,
    who closes and no one shall open,
says this:
    " ' "I know your works (behold, I have left an open door before you,
which no one can close)" ' " (Rev 3:7-8).

Dear Brothers in the Lord,

By just about any measure, Darrell was a character. Diabetes had taken one of his legs a few years before I met him, and various other maladies aggravated his scrawny frame, but he was a man who looked forward in hope and faith. I never asked what crime earned him a sentence on death row, and it wouldn't have mattered. He had already been there more than twenty years, and somewhere along the line, having been disowned by family, he awakened to Christ, who set him free.

During my years in Arkansas I visited death row regularly and usually offered Mass for the Catholic inmates in a tiny room euphemistically referred to as "the chapel." It was in fact an office with a metal desk, three metal folding chairs and a metal storage cabinet. Each time I arrived, I first visited some of the inmates individually, either through the metal bars of their cells or through the small openings used for serving meals. Stacked four stories around a vast, open concrete hall, the cells gave every inmate a bird's eye view of what was happening in their noisy world.

When security arrangements were complete, I would be escorted into the chapel, followed by no more than three inmates, each shackled hands and feet the entire Mass. One served as lector, and after my homily all shared personal reflections on the day's readings. Darrell always had the most to say, and the other inmates always listened. He condensed the Scripture passages to their barest essentials and was invariably on the mark. The others acknowledged him as a kind of grandfather and father-in-faith, both because he had served longer on the Row than anyone else and because he bore authentic witness to Christ. Interminable legal procedures and appeals—long ago exhausted and now in suspended animation—had given Darrell a playful patience with which he worked the system as well as anyone. Here was a man of faith who was no one's fool, and the others looked up to him with good reason.

Darrell and I corresponded between visits, and he was never shy about offering advice or speaking up on behalf of all inmates everywhere. He justifiably identified himself as a prison minister and advocated for the needs of others, be they spiritual, financial, or legal. He once wrote, "Death row ministry is unlike other prison ministry because you don't just help them live, you sometimes have to help them die. . . . You try to meet little needs, listen, let them know you care, help them find some hope for the future. When you don't have any hope for the future there is no joy to be found in the present. I know, I've been there."

Incredibly, Darrell met little needs, listened, let them know he cared, and helped them find hope despite the fact that he rarely left his cell and thus rarely had the opportunity to speak to another inmate face-to-face. He did it all by encouragement and humor shouted through steel bars, notes dragged cell to cell by a piece of string, advice and comfort spread quietly by word of mouth, and small treats such as ice cream shrewdly arranged with the guards. When he died of natural causes, his passing was mourned by all (on the "outside" as well as "inside") who had been encouraged by his faith. More than one of his friends told me that though they missed him, they were glad he was now with God.

On December 20, we prayed at the Magnificat:

> O Key of David, O royal Power of Israel controlling at your will the gate of heaven: come, break down the prison walls of death for those

who dwell in darkness and the shadow of death; and lead your
captive people into freedom.

What struck me most about Darrell was that he had allowed Christ to
be his Key to freedom long before he died. He had regret and deep sorrow, no doubt about it, but they did not imprison him; he was full of
contrition but trusted in God's mercy. So free was he in Christ that he
once told me it was probably better for him to be in prison than outside,
where he would surely get into mischief.

In a letter to his fiancée, Dietrich Bonhoeffer wrote, "A prison cell, in
which one waits, hopes, does various unessential things, and is completely dependent on the fact that the door of freedom has to be opened
from the outside, is not a bad picture of Advent."[1]

The Advent/Christmas season opens us to a deeper realization of our
need for the Savior, our absolute dependence on God's grace and, much
to our exasperation, our resistance to it. There is always another layer
of self-reliance to be peeled away, another stranglehold of selfishness to
be relinquished, another anxiety to be released, another part of life in
need of cleansing: *another door, opened lovingly by Christ, through which to
pass*. Discipleship is about conversion and freedom, both of which are
his work.

Perhaps like me you find New Year's resolutions perilous. And so
perhaps with me you will resolve this coming year simply to move
forward in hope through that door opened by Christ with more childlike
and generous docility to his grace. If we are to make such a resolution,
he will ask us to let go of prejudice, fear, anger, resentment, regret, painful memories, grudges, second-guessing, doubt, hesitation, sinful habits,
judgmentalism, ambition, and the drive to self-sufficiency. *And he will
set us free.*

It might seem strange that I would bring up purgatory in this context,
but these words of Hans Urs von Balthasar have put things in perspective for me:

> Purgatory: perhaps the deepest but also the most blissful kind of
> suffering. The terrible torture of having to settle now all the things
> we have dreaded a whole lifelong. The doors we have frantically
> held shut are now torn open. But all the while this knowledge: now
> for the first time I *will* be able to do it—that ultimate thing in me,
> that total thing. Now I can feel my wings growing; now I am fully
> becoming myself.[2]

"For freedom Christ set us free," writes Paul to the Galatians (5:1). This is a lesson he and Peter had learned firsthand.

Imprisoned by the paranoid Herod, for example, Peter was doubly-chained and doubly-watched, and the prison itself was guarded by four squads of four soldiers each. Talk about overkill! But while sleeping, he was tapped on the side and awakened by the angel of the Lord, the chains fell from his wrists, and he was led to freedom. Freed, he returned to the preaching of the Gospel.

To say the least, Herod's prison precautions were excessive. But is it not equally possible, as von Balthasar suggests, that at times we can just as obsessively and frantically hold shut the doors to our own freedom out of fear or distrust, while the Lord is ready to free us? And in shuttering tight the doors to freedom, might we not be stifling the Lord's proclamation of the Gospel through us?

When God opened the door to freedom in the birth of his Son, he found us clutching all kinds of unessential and hazardous things. Blessed are we when we release our fearful grip on false securities and give them to him. Then we will be free to serve him unfettered and with our whole lives, relying solely on his grace. Then we will be full of joy!

As von Balthasar also suggests, "He desires to empty himself in order that we might receive something."[3] And in another place,

> If anyone—God, for instance—takes away your coat, give him your shirt as well. And if anyone—God, for instance—asks you to go ten miles with him, go the twenty.[4]

It was at his conception in the womb of his mother that God's Son first emptied himself for our sake. Here lies a quiet but essential Christmas message for us priests: When God asks us to "give the shirt as well" and "go the twenty," it is so that we might learn to empty ourselves as did Jesus in the Incarnation and on the Cross. It is in emptying ourselves that we prepare to receive him who has opened the door of our personal captivity. It is in emptying ourselves that we become free for Christ, free in Christ. It is emptying ourselves that we allow God to cleanse us for "that ultimate thing . . . that total thing." It is emptying ourselves that we discover the lightness of freedom, the joy of handing things over to God. It is in emptying ourselves that we prepare to celebrate the Eucharist, preach the Word, and lead our people to him.

One Christmas when I visited Darrell and the other death row inmates, I was not allowed to celebrate Mass because of an all-too-common prison foul-up. Instead I went to the individual cells of my congregation and read Luke's account of the birth of Jesus to each inmate. Darrell took it in stride with a roll of his eyes, accustomed as he was to such unjust inconveniences, and listened attentively to the Christmas gospel as a message of freedom in a place of confinement.

It strikes me that the stable in which Jesus was born had no doors because inside lay perfect freedom. Did he not say that he has left a door open for us, which no one can close? Peter and Paul learned that they were set free to preach Christ, and he indeed opened doors to them— prison doors certainly, but even more importantly, the doors of souls hungering for the Savior. In the next few days, may the Lord open such doors for us, too. Emptying ourselves for him and for those he loves, may we freely preach his Word and lovingly feed his flock by hand.

Sincerely in Christ,

+ *Peter Sartain*

Archbishop Peter Sartain

Notes

1. Dietrich Bonhoeffer, *A Testimony to Freedom: The Essential Writings of Dietrich Bonhoeffer,* edited by Geffrey D. Kelly and F. Burton Nelson (New York: Harper-Collins, 1995), 490.

2. Hans Urs Von Balthasar, *The Grain of Wheat: Aphorisms* (San Francisco: Ignatius Press, 1995), 13.

3. Ibid., 4.

4. Ibid., 9–10.

PRIESTLY PRAYER

21

They Love Our Holiness

Dear Brothers in the Lord,

Karl Frederick Wilhelm Maria Leisner, prisoner 22356, died at age thirty on August 12, 1945—barely three months after the liberation of the Dachau concentration camp. He had been imprisoned for five and a half years.

Born at Rees, Germany, on February 28, 1915, Karl was the eldest of five children. Growing up during the rise of National Socialism, he sensed a call to the priesthood and entered the seminary. But his seminary formation was interrupted by six months of compulsory government service in a labor camp, which entailed back-breaking work in murky swamps.

Six months after diaconate ordination, he was diagnosed with tuberculosis, most likely contracted in the swamps, and was sent to a local sanitarium to regain his health. Hearing of a failed attempt on Hitler's life, he made an offhand comment about the situation to a group of patients and was reported to the local police as harboring anti-Nazi sentiments. He was taken directly from the sanitarium to jail, and thus began five and a half years in the hands of the Nazis: first at Freiburg, then at Mannheim and Sachsenhausen, and finally at Dachau.

Leisner quickly became a favorite of other prisoners. Though sick and deeply affected by the desperate environment of the camps, he was always joyful and encouraged others. Much to the dismay of those who knew him best, he scrounged bits of food for the hungriest and sickest and shared his own meager rations despite needing food as much as anyone else.

Reading *The Victory of Fr. Karl,* I was struck by the way he was treated by his fellow prisoners.[1] They respected and loved him, much as one might love a little brother, but their love was also for something much more profound: *they loved his holiness.* By that I mean something different from admiration and respect. They guarded, protected, and loved his holiness as something essential for their own survival. Loving him, they preserved and nurtured something in and for themselves: hope in God.

Leisner had been imprisoned just months before his ordination to the priesthood, and fellow prisoners shared the unlikely hope that he could be ordained a priest even in the camp. The unthinkable became possible when a French bishop was sentenced to Dachau for his collaboration with the Resistance.

All the necessary documents were smuggled in and out of the camp. At great personal risk, a twenty-year-old woman living in a local convent became an underground courier. In early December 1944, Leisner received a letter from one of his sisters, in the middle of which was written in another's hand: "I authorize the ceremonies requested provided that they are done validly and that there remain of them definite proof." The words were followed by the signature of Leisner's bishop.

Many prisoners participated surreptitiously in an intricate plot to prepare for the ordination. Vestments were tailored for the bishop and Leisner, a bishop's ring was crafted by a Russian communist, and a crozier was carved by a Benedictine monk. Inscribed into the curve of the staff were the words, *Victor in Vinculi* (Victor in Chains).

Still weak with tuberculosis and his face red with fever, Leisner was ordained a priest at Dachau on December 17, 1944. He secretly celebrated his first Mass on December 26, the only Mass he would ever offer.

When the Allies liberated Dachau on April 29, 1945, the gravely ill Leisner was taken to a hospital, where he died on August 12 in the presence of his family. For most of his life he had kept a diary, and the last entry, dated July 25, echoed the final words of St. Stephen: "Bless my enemies, too, O Lord. 'Lord, lay not this sin to their charge.'"

Blessed John Paul II beatified Karl Leisner in 1996 in the Olympic stadium in Berlin, built by Hitler for the 1936 games. He carried the crozier made for Blessed Karl's ordination.

I learned something important when I read Leisner's biography: *God's people love our holiness.* By that I do not mean that they admire holiness from afar, as if we priests are to be holy as a kind of decoration for the Church. Our people's love for our holiness is an active and nurturing love, through which they sustain and encourage something essential both to our vocation and their own spiritual health. They know instinctively that we are called to be holy *for them*. We strive to be holy not *in lieu of* their holiness, but we strive to be holy *for* them, as part of our priestly sacrifice. Everything about us, in fact, is to be *for them*. Just as his fellow prisoners loved Fr. Karl's holiness because they recognized who he was for them, so our people love our holiness and Christian charity and see them as evidence of the kingdom and signs of hope. Moreover, their love for our holiness is a constant reiteration and encouragement of our vocation, as God uses them as his instruments to remind us of who he has called us to be.

In *The Meaning of Christian Priesthood,* Gisbert Greshake suggests that the sacramental character we received at ordination is a "sign of lowliness," a constant reminder that we are merely Christ's "unprofitable servants" (cf. Luke 17:7-10). It is this character that makes it possible to accept the vocation to priesthood without presumption but also without anxiety and embarrassment. Ordination bestows the holiness that is required for priestly action. "Looked at in this way the priestly office which comes from Christ is something 'objectively holy' and 'objectively sanctifying' and in its official sacramental functions it represents Christ and does not depend on the personal holiness of the minister."[2]

Notwithstanding the fact that the effectiveness of the sacraments is not dependent on the holiness of the priest but on the action of Christ, we were called to adopt a way of life through which our vocation becomes visible, credible, and even evangelical. Christ was revealed as the perfect exemplar of vocation: "He is what he does and he does what he is. In his life he is the union of sign and reality, of witness and testimony."[3] Origen called him the *autobasileia*—the kingdom of God in person.

Humbly and without pretense, we must constantly acknowledge interiorly and manifest exteriorly that we are the kingdom of God *in person*, due to the objective holiness conferred upon us through the grace of ordination. We are evidence of his kingdom and signs of hope.

As Cardinal Francis Xavier Van Thuan wrote in *Prayers of Hope, Words of Courage*:

> A sign is a witness. The Lord asks me to be a sign showing the Father in heaven to all people. Perhaps it may happen that to be a witness I must scream like an ambulance siren. . . . But most of the time, a

sign is silent. Often it is sufficient to be present—constantly, obstinately, courageously present—and never leave one's post.[4]

We should never underestimate the sign of the kingdom of God that we are as priests. Our simple, constant, and prayerful presence does more than we can ever imagine. Because God is at work, we are signs of hope in a manner far beyond our capacity and often even beyond our awareness.

I would like to tell you about something I experienced a few years ago. I hesitate to write of this incident because I fear that doing so might seem self-serving. Therefore I must preface it by making clear that it was one of the most jarring and challenging moments of my life.

One night I traveled to Texas for a meeting, arriving late at the hotel hungry and tired. I checked in, went to my room, and then returned to the lobby to ask directions to the nearest fast-food restaurant. The young clerk was helpful, and I headed toward the door. As I was about to exit, he said, "You're one of those holy guys." I smiled. I was wearing a clerical shirt and pectoral cross; it was not difficult to figure out what I do for a living. "Yes, I'm the Catholic bishop of Arkansas, and I'm here for a meeting." "No," he said, "that's not what I meant. I could see it on your face."

He did not know it, but that was one of the most challenging things anyone had ever said to me. He did not say, "I noticed the collar, I noticed the cross, and I know there's a seminary down the street." By saying, "I could see it on your face," he stopped me in my tracks. It was as if God were saying to me, "Disregard what might seem like a compliment and recognize that because you are a priest I am always at work in you. Stay close to me and let me work through you. It is I he just saw, not you."

Every encounter we have each day, no matter its purpose or place, is an encounter of Christ: *we see him* in every person, but in a sacramental way, *in meeting us they are meeting him.* We must never lose sight of that fact of priestly life. It is especially challenging when we deal with troublesome parishioners who do not seem to have our good or even the welfare of the parish at heart. It is not at all easy to keep our wits and the attitude of Christ when faced with those whose intentions are not the best. Even if their behavior is not Christ-like, ours must be.

Our habits, entertainments, conversations, casual comments, and style of life must always conform to Christ in us. Insofar as there is inconsistency we obscure his presence and risk giving scandal to those who seek in us the evidence of what they hope for. That is why our lives should be marked by continual conversion. Conversion brings peace because it brings our lives more into sync with our purpose and destiny—and our vocation.

The reason we feel guilty when we have sinned is because we were not made for sin! Sin is beneath our dignity as human persons, and when we sin a natural kind of dissonance (i.e., guilt) wells up from within. Commenting on Hebrews 4:15 ("For we do not have a high priest who is unable to sympathize with our weaknesses, but one who has similarly been tested in every way, yet without sin"), Raniero Cantalamessa writes:

> The expression "except in sin" . . . does not convey some exception to the full and definitive human nature of Christ, as though he were in all respects fully human like ourselves, less one thing: sin—as though sin were an essential and natural characteristic of human nature. Far from derogating from the full humanity of Christ, "except in sin" constitutes . . . the only spurious addition to the divine project of human nature. It is surprising how we have reached the point of regarding as most "human" the very thing that is least human. "To this point has human perversity arrived," says Saint Augustine, "that he whom lust overcomes is regarded as a man, whereas he who has overcome lust cannot be a man. Those who overcome evil cannot be men, whereas those whom evil overcomes are men indeed!" "Human" has come to mean rather what we have in common with the beasts than what distinguishes us from them, such as intelligence, will, power, conscience, holiness.
>
> So Jesus is "true man" not *in spite of* being without sin but precisely *because* he is without sin.[5]

Conversion brings peace because it brings our lives into sync with our purpose and destiny. Conversion is also a critical part of the witness we as priests are to give those we serve: we are to be signs of hope who doggedly trust in God's transforming power and seek each day to be even clearer signs of the kingdom.

On the one hand, I am humbled and comforted that Christ works in me despite my unworthiness and ineptitude. On the other hand, I see clearly that the indelible sacramental character of ordination is at the same time a call to conversion and personal holiness—so that by his grace there will be less and less a discrepancy between who I am and how I act. The means to answering that call is prayer. Through prayer God breathes the kingdom into me, deeper and deeper, without my even knowing it.

Blessed Karl responded to the call to holiness in settings that make most of our struggles seem small in comparison. But what nourished and sustained him, and the spiritual process that made him holy, are the same for you and me: prayer and love. That is why it is important to keep in mind the *gift of holiness* given us at ordination and our responsibility both to nourish it ourselves and to allow our people to *love the gift at work in us*. Everything about us is to be *for them*, including the hours we spend on our knees and confessing our sins.

We are signs of the kingdom. Every one of our encounters is an encounter of Christ, and in him we are the kingdom of God *in person*. God's power at work in us can do immeasurably more than we can ask or imagine.

Sincerely in Christ,

+ *Peter Sartain*

Archbishop Peter Sartain

Notes

1. Otto Pies, *The Victory of Fr. Karl* (New York: Farrar, Straus and Cudahy, 1957).

2. Gisbert Greshake, *The Meaning of Christian Priesthood* (Dublin: Four Courts Press, 1988), 110.

3. Ibid., 112.

4. Francis Xavier Nguyễn Văn Thuận, *Prayers of Hope, Words of Courage* (Boston: Pauline Books and Media), 24.

5. Raniero Cantalamessa, OFM, *Jesus Christ, the Holy One of God* (Collegeville, MN: Liturgical Press, 1992), 36–37.

22

The Prayer I Hesitate to Pray

Dear Brothers in the Lord,

I have titled this letter "The Prayer I Hesitate to Pray" for a reason.

André Zirnheld was born in Paris in 1913, the son of Alsatian parents who had chosen to live in France in 1870. He studied at the Sorbonne, became a philosophy professor, and eventually joined a French squadron attached to the British SAS (Special Air Service) as a paratrooper. After he was killed in action in Libya in 1942, his fellow paratroopers took inventory of his personal effects. Among them they found a copy of Jacques Maritain's *St. Paul*, a work by Bergson, and a notebook containing this handwritten prayer which Zirnheld had composed in Tunis in April 1938:

Prière (Prayer)

Give me, my God, what you have left.
Give me what no one ever asks of you.
I do not ask you for rest
or tranquility,
neither of soul nor of body.
I do not ask you for wealth
or success or even health.
All of that, my God, people ask of you so much
that you must not have any more.
Give me, my God, what you have left.

Give me what others refuse from you.
I want insecurity and anxiety.
I want storm and strife
and that you would give them to me once and for all, my God,
so that I will be certain of having them always,
since I will not always have the courage
to ask them of you.
Give me, my God, what you have left.
Give me what others do not want.
But give me also courage and strength and faith.
Because you alone, my God, give
that which one cannot expect of oneself.

The few facts I have been able to discover about Zirnheld do not reveal whether he was a particularly religious man, but his prayer is heartfelt and courageous. No doubt spurred by his love for France and his passionate drive for its liberation, the prayer nonetheless touched me deeply as one I too should pray.

I began asking myself: "Has it ever occurred to me to pray such a prayer?" My answer was a spontaneous "no," but I could not get the prayer and its sentiments out of my head. I kept thinking that my prayers are typically for peace of mind, clarity, security, a straight and well-lit path—another way of saying that my prayers are often like most prayers, invoked to avoid suffering. Zirnheld's prayer, however, has challenged me to approach things differently.

A scribe once said to Jesus: "Teacher, I will follow you wherever you go." Jesus responded, "Foxes have dens and birds of the sky have nests, but the Son of Man has nowhere to rest his head" (Matt 8:19-21; Luke 9:57-58). Jesus was a man on the move because he was Emmanuel, God himself who had pitched his tent in the midst of his people and the insecurities that mark their lives. Saint Bernard wrote that Jesus went "so far as to pitch his tent in the sun so even the dimmest eyes see him."[1] But being seen by all was not the end of it. As Emmanuel he was also the servant of all.

> Then the mother of the sons of Zebedee approached him with her sons and did him homage, wishing to ask him for something. He said to her, "What do you wish?" She answered him, "Command that these two sons of mine sit, one at your right and the other at your left, in your kingdom." Jesus said in reply, "You do not know what

you are asking. Can you drink the cup that I am going to drink?" They said to him, "We can." He replied, "My cup you will indeed drink, but to sit at my right and at my left [, this] is not mine to give but is for those for whom it has been prepared by my Father." When the ten heard this, they became indignant at the two brothers. But Jesus summoned them and said, "You know that the rulers of the Gentiles lord it over them, and the great ones make their authority over them felt. But it shall not be so among you. Rather, whoever wishes to be great among you shall be your servant; whoever wishes to be first among you shall be your slave. Just so, the Son of Man did not come to be served but to serve and to give his life as a ransom for many." (Matt 20:20-28)

Grasping something of the kingdom and power of Jesus, the mother of the sons of Zebedee wanted to ensure for her sons a stable position. The other ten disciples, annoyed at the posturing of the two, grumbled about placement and status. Speaking to all twelve, Jesus suggested that the only openings in his kingdom were for servants and slaves. Lordly supervisors need not apply.

At moments of sincere fervor, just like the scribe and the sons of Zebedee, I have said to the Lord: "I will follow you wherever you go. I can drink of your cup!" But later when I found myself at the threshold of a wilderness I had never entered or when I got a true taste of the Lord's cup—I hesitated. Was my earlier fervor a façade? Are my intentions truly those of the reign of Jesus? What could it mean if he has led me into a place of insecurity where the peace he promised is nowhere to be found?

Priestly ministry, pitched as a tent in the midst of the people of God, is beset with paradox upon paradox. On the one hand, we disciples of the Lord are to have no place to lay our heads and are to drink of the cup of his suffering. Insecurity and strife find their way into our schedules on a regular basis. On the other hand, we hear Jesus saying: "Come to me . . . and I will give you rest"; "my peace I give to you"; "Do not be afraid"; "you are worth more than many sparrows"; "Do not let your hearts be troubled. You have faith in God; have faith also in me. . . . I will come back again and take you to myself, so that where I am you also may be" (Matt 11:28; John 14:27; Matt 28:10; Matt 10:31; John 14:1, 3).

I have learned (and am still learning) that rest comes not when the schedule lightens but when I place things squarely in God's hands. Peace comes not when the troubles go away but when I trust in the Father as Jesus did. Fear dissipates not when uncertainties cease but when I remember that all things have been and always will be resolved in God's love. Worthiness is found not in my accomplishments but in God's grace.

My "place" is not a "place" at all but being at the side of Jesus. It is only with those insights that I can dare to pray Zirnheld's prayer.

But what of those "leftovers" for which Zirnheld prayed? Are they somehow less than the best God has to offer, the dregs of what he has freely given to everyone else? I wonder if Zirnheld was thinking about the Syro-Phoenician woman.

> Then Jesus went from that place and withdrew to the region of Tyre and Sidon. And behold, a Canaanite woman of that district came and called out, "Have pity on me, Lord, Son of David! My daughter is tormented by a demon." But he did not say a word in answer to her. His disciples came and asked him, "Send her away, for she keeps calling out after us." He said in reply, "I was sent only to the lost sheep of the house of Israel." But the woman came and did him homage, saying, "Lord, help me." He said in reply, "It is not right to take the food of the children and throw it to the dogs." She said, "Please, Lord, for even the dogs eat the scraps that fall from the table of their masters." Then Jesus said to her in reply, "O woman, great is your faith! Let it be done for you as you wish." And her daughter was healed from that hour. (Matt 15:21-28)

This beautiful exchange demonstrates both Jesus's thirst for faith and the power of what the woman cleverly calls "the scraps." Because Jesus never gives anything but his all, the woman's faith was well placed, and her daughter's healing was complete.

All four gospels report that after Jesus miraculously fed the hungry crowds there were twelve baskets of fragments left. "Scraps" and "fragments" perhaps, but each contained the fullness of Jesus's gift, and each was enough to satisfy all people of all time, including you and me.

Whatever God provides—food and shelter, insecurity and strife, rest and consolation, uncertainty and darkness, position and status, or upheaval and eviction—it is what we need, precisely *because* he gives or allows it, and it is where his grace will be revealed. It will satisfy in a manner and to a degree far beyond our expectation. As John Henry Newman wrote in *Meditations on Christian Doctrine*:

> Therefore I will trust him. Whatever, wherever I am, I can never be thrown away. If I am in sickness, my sickness may serve him; in perplexity, my perplexity may serve him; if I am in sorrow, my sorrow may serve him . . . God does nothing in vain . . . He may take away my friends, he may throw me among strangers, he may make me feel desolate, make my spirits sink, hide the future from me—still he knows what he is about.[2]

It is not at all a bad thing to pray for peace of mind, tranquility, and rest. Who would not want such gifts from the Lord? But perhaps we limit our growth by assuming they come in only one form. I have discovered that this Prayer I Hesitate To Pray helps me look for God where I am, in the circumstances and bread of today, in the insecurity or the stability that now engulfs me, in the feast or fragment set before me at each moment. In many ways, it is the prayer of Jesus on the cross, his trusting abandonment to the care of his Father. It helps me personalize the Words of Institution when I celebrate Mass, as I ask God to help me "give" my life and "shed" my blood with him for his people—each day and once and for all. We priests are united to the One who had nowhere to lay his head, the One from whose cup we drink every day, the One who entered knowingly into the insecurity and strife of human existence—in order to redeem it.

Jesus answered the plea of the mother of the sons of Zebedee. According to tradition, James, son of Zebedee and brother of John, was "the first among the Apostles to drink of Christ's chalice of suffering" (Prayer Over the Offerings, Feast of St. James). No doubt it was not easy in those early days (is it any easier in our own?), but James learned the Lord's way of humility and self-sacrificing love "to the end."

Zirnheld's prayer was adopted by French paratroopers and is now commonly known as *La Prière du Para* (The Paratrooper's Prayer), but I think it could also be called "A Priest's Prayer," because it stretches us to pray as Jesus prays and to love as Jesus loves. I pray for the courage to mean it when I pray it. God alone can give what we cannot expect of ourselves.

Sincerely in Christ,

+ Peter Sartain

Archbishop Peter Sartain

Notes

1. Bernard of Clairvaux, Sermon I in Epiphany, qtd. in the Office of Readings, *The Liturgy of the Hours*, vol. I, trans. the International Commission on English in the Liturgy (New York: Catholic Book Publishing, 1975), 447.

2. John Henry Newman, qtd. in *Prayers, Verses, and Devotions* (San Francisco: Ignatius Press, 2000), 339.

23

On Compunction

Dear Brothers in the Lord,

As Lent progresses, I find myself reflecting more and more on repentance, conversion, what the Lord asks of me—and even more, what he offers me.

> After arresting him they led him away and took him into the house of the high priest; Peter was following at a distance. They lit a fire in the middle of the courtyard and sat around it, and Peter sat down with them. When a maid saw him seated in the light, she looked intently at him and said, "This man too was with him." But he denied it saying, "Woman, I do not know him." A short while later someone else saw him and said, "You too are one of them"; but Peter answered, "My friend, I am not." About an hour later, still another insisted, "Assuredly, this man too was with him, for he also is a Galilean." But Peter said, "My friend, I do not know what you are talking about." Just as he was saying this, the cock crowed, and the Lord turned and looked at Peter; and Peter remembered the word of the Lord, how he had said to him, "Before the cock crows today, you will deny me three times." He went out and began to weep bitterly. (Luke 22:54-62).

Only Luke reports that the Lord "turned and looked at Peter." He doesn't describe the look or explain what it signified. He simply recounts what must have been an excruciatingly painful moment for Peter, who fled the courtyard in bitter tears. A simple glance from the one he loved—the one to whom he had sworn unfailing fidelity but had now betrayed—was enough to turn Peter's world upside down.

Even though Peter might have perceived it at first as a look of condemnation, it was not; Jesus had said he had not come for condemnation. Instead, this was a glance from perfect Love which brought into sharp relief the chasm between Peter's heart and his behavior. It was a great blessing.

Part of the blessing was that Peter returned the glance and looked into Jesus' eyes. I wonder if Peter could ever think back on that moment without tearing up. One thing is clear from his fearless faithfulness to the Lord in the years that followed: he had learned that Jesus, ever faithful, meant what he had said about forgiveness. Having been forgiven seventy times seven times, Peter became more and more a man of mercy. He never forgot that look from Jesus in the high priest's courtyard, and he returned the look again daily in prayer. He lived his life in joyful proclamation and praise of the mercy of Jesus.

I have always been drawn to the ancient Christian concept of "compunction," because it encompasses the inner dynamic we experience when confronting both the depth of our sinfulness and the infinity of God's mercy. Compunction involves a jumble of emotions—heartfelt sorrow for sin, authentic love for the Lord, wearisome embarrassment and frustration at our fickleness, joy in the freedom God has opened for us, unending gratitude, and the urge to live differently in the future. Compunction is the result of looking Jesus in the eye and understanding fully what mercy is.

The effect of compunction is beatitude. Saint John Chrysostom writes, "It is possible to be in mourning for one's own sins and in joy because of Christ."[1] Saint Nilus writes:

> Lamentation over one's sins brings a very sweet sadness and a bitterness which tastes like honey, being seasoned with a marvelous hope. That is why it nourishes the body, causes the depths of the soul to shine with joy, enriches the heart and causes our whole being to thrive. How right David was to sing, "Tears have become my bread day and night." (Psalm 41:4)[2]

And Abba Isaiah writes:

> Sadness according to God . . . is a joy, the joy of seeing yourself in God's will. . . . Sadness according to God does not weigh on the

soul, but says to it, "Do not be afraid! Up! Return!" God knows that man is weak and strengthens him.[3]

Compunction is the amazement of a desperately ill person that he or she has been cured. He or she never forgets the disease and thus never forgets the cure. I think that is what filled Peter's heart for the rest of his life; he would never forget his betrayal, and he would never forget Jesus' forgiveness. Through the glance of Jesus, he saw himself in God's will and became a man of hope and joy and mercy.

One day after she had been to confession, St. Catherine of Siena composed a prayer for the intention of the pope. It reads, in part:

> So I will never stop knocking
> at the door of your kindness,
> my Love,
> asking you to raise him up.
> Reveal your power in him, then,
> so that his fearless heart
> may always burn with your holy desire
> and be seasoned with your humility.
> Let him carry out his actions
> with your kindness
> and charity
> and purity
> and wisdom . . .
> Give him knowledge of your truth within himself
> So that he may know himself in himself—
>   What he used to be—
> And you in himself—by your grace.[4]

Peter saw "himself in himself" when he realized his betrayal, and he saw Jesus in himself by grace when he returned the glance.

Commenting on the passage from Luke, Fr. Jacques Philippe offers a stunning observation:

> Peter broke down in tears, in which his heart was purified there and then. Judas, why did you avoid Jesus' eyes, and so trap yourself in your own despair? Right up until the very end the hope of salvation and forgiveness could have been yours. Your sin was no worse than Peter's. . . .[5]

Do we priests sometimes avoid the glance of Jesus, fearful that it is one of condemnation or anxious because we will have to face the chasm that exists between our heart and our behavior? Do we carry the burden of our sinfulness and all the baggage that piles up alongside it without unburdening ourselves? Do we fail to give Jesus the opportunity to free us from our sins and so remain imprisoned and paralyzed in our shame? Do we neglect the opportunity to be filled with the very mercy he has called us to share with those he loves? Do we go to confession often enough?

It is not enough for a priest to embrace the *concept* of God's mercy. We must *experience and be steeped in* his mercy, filled with the jumble of emotions that mark compunction, fueled with the hope that made Peter bold and unafraid, imbued with the humility that makes us eager to face our sinfulness, and blessed by the glance of Jesus, who helps us know ourselves in his grace. To be good confessors, we must be committed to a life of personal conversion. We must seek God's protection from evil and the grace to avoid sin. We who absolve the sins of others must confess our sins regularly.

I have a feeling that often we have no clue that we are weighed down by our sins. Sadly, we perhaps become so accustomed to the extra weight that we forget the lightness of freedom in God's mercy. We can become hardened and arrogant without realizing it. Perhaps even as we assure others of God's mercy we privately fear that it does not apply to us, and we keep our heads down to avoid the glance of Jesus. Or perhaps we tell ourselves it is difficult to find a confessor, and we do not want to interrupt a brother priest's busy life. We need to *hear* the words of absolution as much as we proclaim them, for the tender love of Jesus is directed our way as well. Saint John Vianney said God is "quicker to forgive than a mother to snatch her child from the fire."[6] Do we allow the Lord to forgive us frequently, to tell us to "rise up" in peace and return, renewed, to his vineyard?

Saint Gregory Nazianzen writes:

> First be purified and then purify others, first allow yourself to be instructed by wisdom and then instruct others, first become light and then enlighten others, first draw close to God and then guide others to him, first be holy yourself and then make others holy.[7]

Let us add: First be freed by Jesus' tender glance of forgiveness and then take his forgiveness to others. He wants us not only to recite the litany of our sins; he wants us to sing the litany of his mercy—by heart.

Brothers in the Lord, may we often turn and look our merciful Jesus in the eyes.

Sincerely in Christ,

+ *Peter Sartain*

Archbishop Peter Sartain

P.S. At the risk of making an already long letter even longer, I want to share with you a beautiful story from the life of St. Jerome that André Louf includes as a postscript in his book, *Tuning into Grace: the Quest for God*. I offer it as a postscript to you as well.

> When believing fifteenth- and sixteenth-century artists wanted to convey an idea of committed faith, they usually referred to a remarkable event in the life of Saint Jerome. Most museums in Flanders, and some churches, have preserved records of it. . . .
>
> Long before he became a learned and famous Bible scholar and flourished on the Aventine in Rome as the spiritual leader of a group of high-society ladies, Jerome had first tried to live the life of a hermit in one of the wadis of the Judean desert, a wadi known even then for its grottoes and caves. This experience was not, however, what he had expected. With the somewhat reckless over-confidence of his age the young Jerome had diligently devoted himself to the many forms of ascesis then practiced by the monks. The benefits, however, escaped him. Time would soon show that his true calling lay elsewhere in the Church and that his stay among the monks in Palestine would be merely prelude to this.
>
> Jerome still had much to learn, for as a young novice he was hopelessly stuck. Despite all his noble efforts, no answering voice came to him from heaven. He drifted directionless on the troubled waters of his mind, so that long-familiar temptations again began to creep up on him incessantly. Jerome lost his courage. Where had he erred? Where lay the cause of this breakdown in his relationship with God?
>
> So Jerome worried and brooded, until suddenly he glimpsed a crucifix that had positioned itself between the dry branches of a dead tree. He threw himself on the ground, beating his breast with firm, sweeping movements. It is in that humble, but at the same time insistent, posture that most painters depict him.
>
> It was not long before Jesus broke the silence and addressed Jerome from the cross.
>
> "Jerome," said he, "what do you have to give me? What am I getting from you?"

That voice alone put fresh heart into Jerome again and he immediately began to wonder what he could offer his crucified friend.

"The loneliness, Lord," he answered. "I offer to you the loneliness with which I am struggling."

"Excellent, Jerome," replied Jesus, "and thank you very much. You have certainly done your best. But have you anything more to give me?"

Not for a minute did Jerome doubt that he had much more to offer Jesus.

"Of course, Lord," he resumed. "My fasting, my hunger and thirst. I only eat after sundown!"

Again Jesus answered: "Excellent, Jerome, and thank you very much. I know it. You have really done your best. But have you anything else to give me?"

Again Jerome reflected on what he might be able to give Jesus. Successively he trotted out his vigils, his long psalmody, his study of the Bible night and day, the celibacy to which he devoted himself as best he could, the lack of conveniences, the poverty, the most unexpected guests he tried to welcome without grumbling and with a not too unfriendly face, and finally the heat of the day and the chill of the night.

Each time Jesus congratulated and thanked him. He had known for a long time that Jerome meant very well.

But with a half-smile on his lips, he also persisted with his questions, asking for more: "Jerome, is there nothing else you can give me? Or is this all?"

At long last Jerome had summed up all the good things he was able to scrape together from his memory. So when Jesus asked the question one more time he had no choice but, in great perplexity and almost total defeat to protest: "But, Lord, have I not given you everything? I have nothing further to offer."

Then Jesus replied—and it became deathly quiet in the hermitage and in the whole Judean wilderness—and said: "But you do, Jerome. You have forgotten something: you must also give me your sins, that I may forgive them."[8]

Notes

1. Qtd. in Irénée Hausherr, *Penthos: The Doctrine of Compunction in the Christian East* (Collegeville: Cistercian Publications, 1982), 140.

2. Qtd. in ibid., 141.

3. Qtd. in ibid.

4. *The Prayers of Catherine of Siena,* edited and translated by Suzanne Noffke, OP (Lincoln: Authors Choice Press, 2001), 257–58.

5. Jacques Philippe, *Interior Freedom* (New York: Scepter Publishers, 2007), 100.

6. Qtd. in Frederick L. Miller, *The Grace of Ars: Reflections on the Life and Spirituality of St. John Vianney* (San Francisco: Ignatius Press, 2010), 196.

7. Gregory Nazianzen, qtd. in Pope John Paul II, *Pastores Gregis,* Post-Synodal Apostolic Exhortation on the Bishop (October 16, 2003), 12.

8. André Louf, *Tuning into Grace: the Quest for God* (Collegeville, MN: Cistercian Publications, 1992), 146–48.

24

Footnotes of the Spiritual Life

foot·note (fo͝ot'nōt') *n.* **1.** Abrv. **fn.** A note placed at the bottom of a page of a book or manuscript that comments on or cites a reference for a designated part of the text. **2.** Something said or done after the more important work has been completed; an afterthought. *–tr.v.* **footnoted, -noting, -notes. 3.** To add further support or evidence for (a statement or opinion, for example).[1]

Dear Brothers in the Lord,

Much of the spiritual life—much of ministry—much of life—is about paying attention to the footnotes.

Of the many conversions I have experienced through the years, one has to do with reading. I hated to read as a kid and did all in my power to avoid it. When reading was required for school, I did the minimum amount required. When it came to more scholarly books, I glossed over footnotes as so much wasted ink, concluding that if what they contained had been important it would have been placed in the body of the text. Besides, skipping footnotes made reading faster.

Much to my surprise, in college I discovered that reading is enjoyable. I began reading books that were not required—newspaper and magazine articles simply because they were interesting, and classic works of literature simply because they were beautiful. When I traveled or anticipated a long wait in the doctor's office, I took a book along for the ride.

I also began paying attention to footnotes. I found that an intriguing idea or an interesting sentence was often followed by a tiny number which directed me to the bottom of the page. More often than not, I found myself pursuing that number. And I found that the footnote frequently led me to another book more interesting than the one I was reading, to an idea more intriguing than the one that had originally grabbed my attention, and—most importantly—to something I needed to know.

I found this to be true of history books, theology books, biographical books, and especially of books about the spiritual life. A particular sentence would speak to me more than others, as if that one sentence was the reason I was reading the book. The thought it conveyed stuck with me as a kind of key that opened other doors, brought new insights, and whetted my appetite for more. At times such thoughts challenged me in ways I had not yet considered and awakened me to changes necessary in my life.

More and more insights unfolded, my hunger grew, and I realized how much more I had to learn, wanted to learn, and needed to learn. I often discovered what I now consider my favorite books simply by pursuing a footnote, and I have often had a sense that God was behind a footnote, inviting me to pay closer attention.

Wives, husbands, fathers, and mothers know well that much of family life is about paying attention to the footnotes. They are so instinctively attuned to their loved ones that even the most subtle of facial expressions or postures, the slightest verbal hint or uncharacteristic silence, speaks volumes. Giving attention to this kind of understated tip-off, they are able to discover what a loved one needs. If they ever stop doing so, family communication disintegrates.

So it is in our relationship with God, and that is why ancient spiritual teachers spoke constantly about the need for "vigilance." God is always communicating with us, but his communication is often understated and subtle. He does not play cat-and-mouse with us, but he does want us to pay attention to the footnotes in our path: the presence, words, needs and love of others; the lessons we learn; the hungers in our hearts; the crosses we carry; our need for his mercy; the poor at the door; the suggestions he plants on our path; and perhaps even the tiny numbers that lead us to the bottom of a page.

Abba Poemen often said, "We do not need anything except a vigilant spirit." For the Abbas and Ammas of the desert, the prayer of quiet was closely related to vigilance, the constant remembrance of God. Monks were encouraged to be on guard first and foremost for the nearness of

God but also for the shrewd ploys of the devil, who was eager to lure them from their cells and away from God.

> An old man said, "Just as no one can cause harm to someone who is close to the king, no more can Satan do anything to us if our souls are close to God, for truly he said, 'Draw near to me, and I shall be near to you.' But since we often exalt ourselves, the enemy has no difficulty in drawing our poor souls into shameful passions."[2]

Vigilance is also a constant theme in the Scriptures. The prophets, realizing that God was "hidden" and could not be called down at their whim, understood that it was for them to wait for God to reveal himself. The psalmist waits for the Lord, keeping vigil by day and by night. Jesus urges his hearers to be watchful and ready, since we do not know the day or the hour. The theme of vigilance reinforces this need to be ready for the self-revelation of God, whenever it might occur.

Just as the prayer of quiet disposes us to vigilance for God's self-revelation, so does it make us aware of our own behavior and the ways in which our daily lives are consistent or inconsistent with God's presence.

> An old man said, "If the inner man is not vigilant, it is not possible to guard the outer man."[3]

Vigilance, as much as it entails careful attention to subtle hints, also entails spontaneity, the readiness to let go of predetermined plans and preferences in favor of God's providence. For those of us accustomed to forming and following our own devices, prayerful vigilance disposes us to abandon them when God unveils a greater, more immediate priority for our time and our love. When he points to one of his own in need, we will not say, "I have plans. I have something more important to do."

None of this is to say that we should be preoccupied or anxious about every small detail of life in order to tease out its deepest meaning or discern every small step. To the contrary, God does not want us to be filled with anxiety. The way to ensure that in the midst of what life gives us we are paying attention to God and not fretting about the small stuff is to surrender all of it to prayer. God will help us separate wheat and chaff. He will help us catch his message.

In flight from the angry Jezebel, Elijah took shelter in a cave of Mount Horeb but was told by the Lord to stand outside and await his passing. Spectacular as they were, neither a strong and heavy wind nor a violent earthquake nor a sizzling fire was a signal that the Lord had come. Instead, a tiny whispering sound announced the Lord's presence. A footnote.

The attentiveness we give God in prayer overflows to daily life, for in prayer he opens our ears, expands our hearts, sharpens our instincts of love, and inspires us to reach beyond ourselves. Ironically and providentially, God can do this whether or not we are disturbed by distractions when we pray. Most importantly, he does it without our even being aware that he is at work deep within. Whereas we worry about fine-tuning our thoughts, God is concerned with fine-tuning our souls.

The crucial correlative to vigilance—the very reason we should be vigilant—is that God is vigilant for us. He continuously loves us, watches us, and attentively cares for us. Were he to stop, we would cease to exist. Simone Weil once wrote, "Why should I have anxiety? It is not my business to think about myself. My business is to think about God. It is for God to think about me."[4] In the same vein, Abraham Heschel suggested:

> The purpose of prayer is to be brought to His attention, to be listened to, to be understood by Him; not to know Him, but to *be known* to Him. To pray is to behold life not only as a result of His power, but as a concern of His will. . . . For the ultimate aspiration of man is not to be a master, but an object of His knowledge. To live "in the light of His countenance," to become a thought of God—that is the true career of man.[5]

In the end, our vigilance puts us in touch with God's vigilance for us, and he shares with us his knowledge of us. In his classic book on the Eucharist, Louis Bouyer wrote that in prayer, everything

> takes on its meaning in our knowledge of God as the one who first knows us. Before we have any consciousness of anything, before we exist, he knows us. He knows us with a knowledge that is love. Once we discover it, all things become resolved in his love.[6]

Prayer is recognition that God keeps vigilant watch over us. We seek to know him and ourselves better by coming into contact with his knowledge and love of us.

As prayer matures, we begin to notice that God guides us to pay attention to the footnotes he sends our way in the course of the day. Thus does he sensitize us to the needs of those around us. Thus does he call us to deeper conversion. Thus does he make us more compassionate. Thus does he teach us to love. Thus does he spur our growth. Thus does he reveal to us what we need to know. Thus does he clarify our understanding of his Word. Thus does he make our hunger for him grow. Thus does he reveal his presence in a whisper. Thus does he send us forth as living signs of his love.

Sincerely in Christ,

+ *Peter Sartain*

Archbishop Peter Sartain

vig·i·lance (vijələns) n. **1.** A state of watchfulness, alertness; **2.** Readiness to meet God at every moment, based on confidence that he is vigilant for us and communicates with us, and our willingness to act spontaneously on his communication; **3.** Awareness that there is much more to daily encounters than meets the eye; **4.** Belief that God speaks in the softest of whispers; **5.** Our receptivity to God's footnotes.

Notes

1. *The American Heritage Dictionary of the English Language* (New York: American Heritage Publishing, 1969), 512.

2. Qtd. in Benedicta Ward, *The Wisdom of the Desert Fathers* (Collegeville: Cistercian Publications, 2006), 39–40.

3. Ibid., 40.

4. Simone Weil, *Waiting for God* (New York: Harper & Row, 1973), 50–51.

5. Abraham Joshua Heschel, *I Asked for Wonder* (New York: Crossroad, 1987), 27.

6. Louis Bouyer, *The Eucharist* (South Bend, IL: University of Notre Dame Press, 1989), 93.

25

A Single Deed, a Single Word, a Single Thought

Dear Brothers in the Lord,

We can never underestimate the power of God's grace hidden in one opportunity, one moment, one word, one thought, one act of love.

A certain day several years ago was particularly difficult and emotionally draining for me. I spent much of that day on the highways of Arkansas, and by midafternoon my gas tank was nearing empty. Seeing a sign for a filling station, I took the next exit. After filling my tank, I went inside the tiny convenience store to pay, entirely preoccupied by the concerns that weighed heavily on me. My worry must have shown. After I signed the credit slip, the man at the cash register said, "Would you like some water?" I hadn't planned to buy water, but it seemed like a good idea. He reached behind the counter, opened the cooler, and handed me a bottle of water. Taking out my wallet, I handed him a five-dollar bill. "No," he said. "This is on me. I figure you guys work hard and need a break now and then."

I thanked him for his unexpected kindness, and as I walked away I thought to myself, "What a nice guy." But before I reached my car, something hit me like a ton of bricks:

> And whoever gives only a cup of cold water to one of these little ones to drink because he is a disciple—amen, I say to you, he will surely not lose his reward. (Matt 10:42)

I literally stopped in my tracks, recognizing that God had extended his consolation, his loving kindness, to me—one of his little ones, a disciple—through the simple deed of a stranger. The day was still tough, but I continued my journey with a peaceful realization that God was accompanying me. All it took was one drink of cold water.

The question is asked in the Talmud: Why was the human race created as a single human being as opposed to the animals, who were created *en masse*? The response comes in Sanhedrin 4:8 (37a): "Whoever destroys a soul, it is considered as if he destroyed an entire world. And whoever saves a life, it is considered as if he saved an entire world." The meaning is that just as when Adam was created he was the entire human population of the world, so we should see each individual as if he or she were the entire population of the world. Thus, if one saves a life it is as if the entire world has been saved.

The teaching reminds us of the sacredness of the individual lives we encounter moment by moment and the opportunities presented us to strengthen and lift them up—*to give them life*. It was an essential part of Mother Teresa's inspiration—to the dismay of those who misunderstood her—that her sisters do not work for social change through conventional methods but by loving one person at a time.

Saint Thérèse of Lisieux, realizing that in the monastery she would not be able to perform great, heroic acts, writes:

> Great deeds are forbidden me. . . . Love proves itself by deeds, so how am I to show my love? . . . The only way I can prove my love is by scattering flowers, and these flowers are every little sacrifice, every glance and word, and the doing of the least actions for love.[1]

She began to see the numerous opportunities for love that confronted her in the lives of the sisters with whom she lived and strove to seize each one, no matter how small. Each act of love was the giving of a widow's mite.

> [Jesus] sat down opposite the treasury and observed how the crowd put money into the treasury. Many rich people put in large sums. A poor widow also came and put in two small coins worth a few cents. Calling his disciples to himself, he said to them, "Amen, I say to you, this poor widow put in more than all the other contributors to the treasury. For they have all contributed from their surplus wealth, but she, from her poverty, has contributed all she had, her whole livelihood." (Mark 12:41-44)

When performed because of Christ and in union with Christ, simple, singular deeds bear power far greater and love much deeper than our own.

Despite Jesus' admonition, many of us fall into the trap of assuming that more words mean more sincere or more effective prayer. "In praying, do not babble like the pagans, who think that they will be heard because of their many words [*polylogia*]" (Matt 6:7). He tells us not to "babble like the pagans," but still we babble like the pagans. We may presume that the more we talk, the louder we talk, the more likely God will hear and answer—as if he could be manipulated in that way. To reduce words in prayer—even to a single word—is a sign of trust in God's loving providence, an act of surrender, and an admission of God's sovereignty and our powerlessness.

In *The Ladder of Divine Ascent*, the seventh-century monk St. John Climacus advises:

> Pray in all simplicity. The publican and the prodigal son were reconciled to God by a single utterance. . . . In your prayers there is no need for high-flown words, for it is the simple and unsophisticated babblings of children that have often won the heart of the Father in heaven. Try not to talk excessively in your prayer, in case your mind is distracted by the search for words. One word from the publican sufficed to placate God, and a single utterance saved the thief. Talkative prayer frequently distracts the mind and deludes it, whereas brevity makes for concentration. If it happens that, as you pray, some word evokes delight or remorse within you, linger over it; for our guardian angel is praying with us.[2]

John contrasts "talkative prayer" (*polylogia*) with "brevity" (*monologia*) and reminds us that even one word touches God's heart. Moreover, praying simply helps break down any illusion that the "power of prayer" is "our" power. Like Naaman the Syrian in 2 Kings 5, we presume that something so simple may not be as effective, and like him we need to learn to surrender to the one God. A single-word prayer exposes the true state of affairs before God: our one-word poverty reveals his lavish bounty.

Saint Clement suggests that when we have sinned, a single heartfelt word suffices to express repentance. He combines quotations from Isaiah and Ezekiel when he writes:

> "As I live," says the Lord, "I do not wish the death of the sinner but his repentance." He added this evidence of his goodness: "House

of Israel, repent of your wickedness. Tell the sons of my people: If their sins should reach from earth to heaven, if they are brighter than scarlet and blacker than sackcloth, you need only turn to me with your whole heart and say, "Father," and I will listen to you as to a holy people."[3]

Even as we pour out our sorrow to God for having sinned, one word breaks through our pain and reaches his merciful heart.

A single deed is one thing. A single word of prayer is another. But what about the power of a single thought?

Saint John of the Cross writes, "One thought alone [*un solo pensamiento*] of man is worth more than the entire world, hence God alone is worthy of it."[4] Ever since I came across this maxim in his *Sayings of Light and Love,* I have kept it in my chapel. A single thought of mine is worth more than the world? A single thought of mine belongs to God? A single thought of mine can give him praise? God does not ask for much, and the extraordinary truth is that every single moment of our existence can be directed toward him and through him to others. Each thought means the world to him.

† † †

Be at peace, brothers in the Lord. Whatever might be burdening you as you read this letter is securely in the Lord's hands. In a simple act of trust, unburden yourself and give the weight to him. He accompanies you as you make it through today.

If your efforts in the parish seem to fall short today, remember that the widow's two coins were worth more than all other contributions combined.

If your faith feels small today, remember that even a mustard seed of faith works wonders.

If the tasks on your plate are more than you can handle, do what you can, simply, and with love.

If the demands of parish life sap your energy and exceed the number of hours in a day, love your parishioners one at a time. By such simple love, directed to the one before you at each moment, lives are saved.

If it seems impossible to pray today, give God one word—your word of love, however it is best expressed—and know that it suffices to touch his heart.

If your sinfulness weighs you down, discourages you, and paralyzes you today, with all your heart turn to God and say, "Father," and he will flood you with mercy.

If your mind is anxious to distraction with haphazard, unmanageable thoughts, remember that a single one of them directed toward God means the world to him.

And keep your eyes open for the one who offers you just a drink of cool water, in whatever form it comes. It is the Lord himself saying, "I am with you, my little one, my disciple."

Sincerely in Christ,

+ *Peter Sartain*

Archbishop Peter Sartain

Notes

1. *The Story of a Soul: The Autobiography of Saint Therese of Lisieux*, trans. John Beevers (New York: Doubleday, 2001), 163.

2. John Climacus, *The Ladder of Divine Ascent,* The Classics of Western Spirituality (New York: Paulist Press, 1982), 275–76.

3. Pope St. Clement, *A Letter to the Corinthians.* Second Reading for Ash Wednesday, *The Liturgy of the Hours,* translated by the International Commission on English in the Liturgy, vol. II (New York: Catholic Book Publishing, 1976), 51–52.

4. *The Collected Works of St. John of the Cross,* translated by Kieran Kavanaugh, OCD, and Otilio Rodriguez, OCD (Washington, DC: Institute of Carmelite Studies, 1979), 670.

26

And There Was Great Calm

Dear Brothers in the Lord,

On the following page is reproduced a photograph of a painting that hangs in my home. Several years ago I asked a friend, a professional artist and the son of one my college philosophy professors, to paint a depiction of Mark 4:35-39.

> On that day, as evening drew on, he said to them, "Let us cross to the other side." Leaving the crowd, they took him with them in the boat just as he was. And other boats were with him. A violent squall came up and waves were breaking over the boat, so that it was already filling up. Jesus was in the stern, asleep on a cushion. They woke him and said to him, "Teacher, do you not care that we are perishing?" He woke up, rebuked the wind, and said to the sea, "Quiet! Be still!" The wind ceased and there was great calm.

Many iconographers and artists through the centuries have offered interpretations of this dramatic scene. Some depict Jesus, hand outstretched, calming the storm. Others, as in my friend's panting, depict him at rest on a cushion. It is an image I love to ponder. When I feel overwhelmed by raging storms and when worrisome thoughts keep me awake at night, I have found consolation in the image of the Lord sound asleep in a storm, resting peacefully and trustingly in his Father.

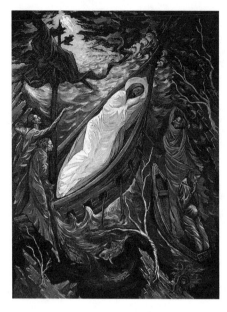

Nick Ring, *Jesus Sleeps in the Storm*,
2005. Acrylic on panel, 48 x 36 inches.
Private collection. Used by permission.

"My soul, be at rest in God alone,
    from whom comes my salvation." (Ps 62:6)

The things that make our stomachs churn and keep us awake at night
vary from person to person, perhaps from year to year or day to day.
The Lord himself asked, "Can any of you by worrying add a single moment to your life-span?" (Matt 6:27), and yet we worry, toss and turn.
We can even be plagued by taunts of the subtle but powerfully haunting
premise that worrying helps us maintain control over a situation, or even
that worrying is our responsibility (as if handing things over to the Lord
would be tantamount to abdicating a responsibility). But unless we let
go of the illusion of control, unless we deliberately abandon everything
to the hands of God, we will not be at rest.

Cast all your worries upon him because he cares for you. (1 Pet 5:7)

A friend once decided to take tennis lessons, the latest in a series of
sports and hobbies he would take up enthusiastically but temporarily
before passing on to another. During his tennis months he would often

quote his coach, referring to his swing: "You have to follow through." We kidded him about his interminable coaching tips, but it occurred to me one day that I was not "following through" when casting my worries on God. My swing, my cast, was incomplete because I refused to let go of control, lest God somehow not do his part. I still have to remind myself often to "follow through" when placing things in God's hands.

> Jesus, looking at him, loved him and said to him, "You are lacking in one thing." (Mark 10:21)

Jesus once encountered a young man who refused to abandon his riches to the kingdom of God. Mark uses the incident to teach that the man's riches had become an obstacle to his acceptance of the kingdom like a little child. Most of us are not wealthy, yet perhaps there is one more thing the Lord calls us to do—to give everything to him each night, that we might rest. He says to us, "Go and give your cares, your worries, your frustrations, and your sins to my Father like a little child, then, come follow me. Then, sleep in peace."

> Rather, I have stilled my soul,
> Like a weaned child to its mother,
>   weaned is my soul.
> Israel, hope in the LORD,
>   now and forever. (Ps 131:2-3)

Everyone is familiar with the story of the nightly prayer of Blessed John XXIII. His private secretary, Msgr. Loris Capovilla, related that each night about midnight, John knelt before the Tabernacle and reflected on the challenges of the day, dizzying in their complexity and variety. He examined his conscience to determine if he had responded appropriately to each. Finally he took a deep breath and said, "Well, I did the best I could. It is your Church, Lord! I'm going to bed. Good night." Like a child, he followed through and abandoned all into the lap of God, resting trustingly in the depths of God's care.

> On hearing that it was Jesus of Nazareth, he began to cry out and say, "Jesus, son of David, have pity on me." (Mark 10:47)

I find that praying simply the name of Jesus throughout the day and when my mind churns at night brings me focus and peace. It is because of him that I am who I am. It is for him that I give myself at each moment. It is to him that all my tasks are directed. It is from him that they receive their inspiration and in him that they will be completed. It is in him that I live and move and have my being. It is his word that I speak, his souls I am sent to shepherd. I am a steward, a useless servant given the awesome privilege of bearing his gifts. To say, again and again, "Jesus," is to abide in his presence and breathe in his peace.

> "Peace I leave with you; my peace I give to you. Not as the world gives do I give it to you. Do not let your hearts be troubled or afraid." (John 14:27)

We repeat these words of the Lord every day at Mass, but I wonder if we see them as having the same effect as his command to the wind and the sea: "Quiet! Be still!" If *his* peace is his gift to us—the peace that allowed him to sleep soundly on a stormy sea—then we, too, can rest in the storm, confident with him that his Father has everything under control.

Blessed John Henry Newman's poem, "Lead, Kindly Light," seems a fitting way to end this letter.

> Lead, kindly Light, amid the encircling gloom,
> Lead Thou me on!
> The night is dark, and I am far from home—
> Lead Thou me on!
> Keep Thou my feet; I do not ask to see
> The distant scene—one step enough for me.
> I was not ever thus, nor prayed that Thou
> Shouldst lead me on.
> I loved to choose and see my path; but now,
> Lead Thou me on!
> I loved the garish day, and, spite of fears,
> Pride ruled my will: remember not past years.
> So long Thy power hath blessed me, sure it still
> Will lead me on,
> O'er moor and fen, o'er crag and torrent, till
> The night is gone;

And with the morn those angel faces smile
Which I have loved long since, and lost awhile.

Sincerely in Christ,

+ *Peter Sartain*

Archbishop Peter Sartain

27

The Way of Peace

Dear Brothers in the Lord,

I doubt any of us accepted the call to priesthood because we were hungry for power. If there were any such hunger pangs in our early response to God, or any traces of them left after ordination, they were quickly dispelled by the reality of our powerlessness. Or were they?

I am often mystified and a little perturbed when I hear people describe priesthood in terms of practical power. Perhaps such misunderstanding has come about because some priests have at times misused our vocation by exercising power in a non-priestly way, giving rise to the hurt and anger of some and the envy of others. Perhaps it has arisen from a secular interpretation of the Church as an institution. Perhaps it is the product of basic human frailty.

Anyone who seeks to live the priestly life hears Jesus teach a lesson vastly different from the hunger for power. After the mother of the sons of Zebedee had asked him for favored status for her sons, Jesus told the apostles:

> "You know that the rulers of the Gentiles lord it over them, and the great ones make their authority over them felt. But it shall not be so among you. Rather, whoever wishes to be great among you shall be your servant; whoever wishes to be first among you shall be your

slave. Just so, the Son of Man did not come to be served but to serve and to give his life as a ransom for many." (Matt 20:20-28)

This was but the tip of the iceberg of Jesus' teaching about sacrificial love, humility, the behavior expected of his disciples, and the true nature of Christian "power" and "authority."

We take these words to heart and try our best to serve humbly. Still, we can't help but confront them time and again because of our powerlessness to fix the situations that life brings our way. Paul, for example, hungered painfully for power over his thorn in the flesh, but through it the Lord taught him an essential lesson:

> that I might not become too elated, a thorn in the flesh was given to me, an angel of Satan, to beat me, to keep me from being too elated. Three times I begged the Lord about this, that it might leave me, but he said to me, "My grace is sufficient for you, for power is made perfect in weakness." I will rather boast most gladly of my weaknesses, in order that the power of Christ may dwell with me. Therefore, I am content with weaknesses, insults, hardships, persecutions, and constraints, for the sake of Christ; for when I am weak, then I am strong. (2 Cor 12:7-10)

The lesson is at the same time beautiful, consoling, and difficult. It is absolutely essential for a peace-filled priestly life.

There is another aspect of that struggle with power, an inner struggle that can manifest itself in the way we deal with conflict.

Not many days—perhaps not many hours—pass in the course of ministry before we are confronted with anger, disappointment, or what we consider an unreasonable expectation. Even though the root of the situation may not be a struggle for power, the dynamic between us and the other might elicit from both them and us a knee-jerk scuffle for comeuppance, power, and control. How will we respond?

Most of us feel a surge of adrenaline when faced with conflict. Our mouths parch, our faces flush, and our bodies tighten with tension. If we feel somehow personally attacked, our first reaction might be to defend ourselves or to attack just as vehemently in return. But no matter the motive or tactic of the other, if we allow the impulse "to win" to control our response, everyone loses. And we have failed to walk the Way of Jesus.

Lent reveals that Way to us.

The Lord GOD has given me
   a well-trained tongue,
That I might know how to answer the weary
   a word that will waken them.
Morning after morning
   he wakens my ear to hear as disciples do;
The Lord GOD opened my ear;
   I did not refuse,
   did not turn away.
I gave my back to those who beat me,
   my cheeks to those who tore out my beard;
My face I did not hide
   from insults and spitting.

The Lord GOD is my help;
   therefore I am not disgraced;
Therefore I have set my face like flint,
   knowing that I shall not be put to shame. (Isa 50:4-7)

Christ also suffered for you, leaving you an example that you should follow in his footsteps.
   "He commited no sin,
   and no deceit was found in his mouth."
When he was insulted, he returned no insult; when he suffered, he did not threaten; instead he handed himself over to the one who judges justly. (1 Pet 2:21-23)

His disciples realized what was about to happen, and they asked, "Lord, shall we strike with a sword?" And one of them struck the high priest's servant and cut off his right ear. But Jesus said in reply, "Stop, no more of this!" (Luke 22:49-51)

Jesus knew that wielding power gets us nowhere, whether that power is expressed in the violence of words, revenge, grudges, or the sword. To the contrary, wielding power perpetuates the cycle of sin he came to break. To endlessly engage in conflict, to allow it to endlessly enslave our emotions, is to give evil its power. Even if the other wants to continue the fight, we must put down the sword.

Jesus said, "Stop, no more of this!"

All of us have the right to discuss with trusted confidantes how to resolve conflicts peacefully. Not to do so can press our anger deep within where it does real damage and from whence it will erupt again, unpredictably and with even greater (and unhealthy) force. It can be helpful to laugh about our conflicts, because a good sense of humor can literally disarm us when our fists are clinched. Sarcasm, however—even sarcasm privately expressed to our confidante—can be just another way to express contempt with no desire for healing.

Spiritually speaking, finding a better way to handle conflict is not first and foremost about learning new skills. It is first about leaning into God.

The "well-trained tongue" of Isaiah's Suffering Servant had been trained by prayer, for it was in prayer "morning after morning" that he learned that the Lord God was his help. Jesus did not hurl insults at those who insulted him but instead delivered himself to his Father, the Just Judge. Knowing that he was doing the Father's will, he did not need to forcefully defend himself against anyone else or be defended forcefully by others. When a disciple used violence to protect him, he said enough was enough.

Inevitably, we will face situations that call for clear, even firm, words; but such words can be spoken without rancor and with peace. Regardless of the motive or tactic of the other, if we allow the impulse "to win" to control our response, everyone loses. When angry, we can pause for a few moments (or even a few days?) to ask the Lord to open our ears to his guidance.

We must not forget that Satan is a terrorist who roams about picking fights. He eggs us on with delight and spins mischief in our parishes and with our inner calm, in order to distract us from the work of the Lord—and the love of the Lord.

> Be sober and vigilant. Your opponent the devil is prowling like a roaring lion looking for [someone] to devour. Resist him, steadfast in faith, knowing that your fellow believers throughout the world undergo the same sufferings. The God of all grace who called you to his eternal glory through Christ [Jesus] will himself restore, confirm, strengthen, and establish you after you have suffered a little. (1 Pet 5:8-10)

It's no accident that the Liturgy of the Hours gives us that passage on Tuesday and the following passage on Wednesday for Night Prayer:

> Be angry but do not sin; do not let the sun set on your anger, and do not leave room for the devil. (Eph 4:26-27)

Jesus' farewell gift was a servant's gift of peace, without any trace of self-justification or retaliation. At a moment of frenzied chaos, he touched the servant's severed ear and healed him. So will he do in the moments of heat we face, if we drop our swords to the ground and "morning after morning" lean with him into his Father. It was with the power of peace that he defeated Satan. As his priests, our way, too, is peace.

Sincerely in Christ,

+ *Peter Sartain*

Archbishop Peter Sartain

28

It Is What It Is

Dear Brothers in the Lord,

Many of us remember that Walter Cronkite ended each night's broadcast of the *CBS Evening News* with the confident statement, "And that's the way it is," followed by the date. Television news was simpler in those days, and in some respects we took it for granted that if The Most Trusted Man in America said that's the way it was, then that was indeed the way it was.

A similar phrase crept into casual conversation a few years back: "It is what it is." Voted by *USA Today* as the "The Sports Quote of 2004," this cliché means: "That's the way it is, we can't change it, and we might as well deal with it."

Much of life involves navigating through situations "as they are." In fact, many of our hours of prayer and ministry are spent trying to understand things as they are, interpreting our personal reactions, confronting our disappointments, opening ourselves sincerely and patiently to God's wisdom—and walking with our parishioners as they do the same. We know well that often there is no answer to the questions "Why?" or "Who's to blame?" That's just the way things are.

When we fail to accept life as it is, our frustration can get the best of us, sour our ministry, embitter us, stunt our spiritual growth, slow our love, and suffocate our joy. We begin to make progress when we accept the statement of the obvious and move beyond it. That is not to say that we like things as they are, that we caused them to be as they are, that we should throw up our hands in defeat and despair, or that things cannot get better. They can get better, and we should take hopeful steps in that direction.

The task is to accept life as it is and offer it to God, that he might shed light on it. Better yet: the task is to trust that life as it is has already been offered by the Lord on the cross.

I have often reflected on the fact that in the incarnation, the Son of God entered the world "as it is," on its own terms, and took everything in his arms to the cross as an offering to the Father. Frustrated, stunted, confused and deceived by original sin, creation had been stuck on itself and in itself, having strayed from its purpose and destiny. Only another divine act could re-create the world as God intended and give us hope when life seems to have become an un-scalable brick wall. God knew that only when we surrender to his wisdom ("mysterious" and "hidden," as Paul writes in 1 Cor 2:7) would we see light when life perplexes, frightens, or discourages.

> I consider that the sufferings of this present time are as nothing compared with the glory to be revealed for us. For creation awaits with eager expectation the revelation of the children of God; for creation was made subject to futility, not of its own accord but because of the one who subjected it, in hope that creation itself would be set free from slavery to corruption and share in the glorious freedom of the children of God. We know that all creation is groaning in labor pains even until now; and not only that, but we ourselves, who have the firstfruits of the Spirit, we also groan within ourselves as we wait for adoption, the redemption of our bodies. For in hope we were saved. Now hope that sees for itself is not hope. For who hopes for what one sees? But if we hope for what we do not see, we wait with endurance. (Rom 8:18-25)

I like Paul's image of creation groaning in labor pains, because in my experience the groaning can be palpable. Haven't we all heard and felt it when comforting parishioners at times of unspeakable tragedy? I like the concept of "subjection to futility," because life as it is can sprout situations that seem disjointed and without purpose. Haven't we sat with friends and brother priests, asking if our efforts have borne any fruit, seeking the energy or courage to get unstuck and move forward?

But labor pains anticipate birth, and subjection gives way to freedom, for those who hope and wait for God.

Perhaps we sometimes regard life as a series of unconnected experiences—some good, some bad—which somehow add up to make our life as it is. We wish some things were different, we regret other things, we cherish many things, we hope for even more—all the while failing to recognize that Christ is at work through everything life brings our way. He is there, within us and around us, above and beneath us, with a love that knits us together as a whole offering that is truly acceptable to the Father. We can take consolation in the fact that everything we experience has already been embraced by the Lord and carried to Calvary. When we allow him to shed upon us the piercing light of his gaze from the cross, we still may not understand everything, but we will know that he does—and that is what matters.

Thus our preaching involves not straining to explain life and its intricacies to our parishioners but proclaiming God's Word so that his light will shine on them, so that they will see how they, too, were in the Lord's heart as he carried the cross. They will be inspired to hope in his love in the midst of life as it is for them. Only he sees life fully and completely as it is.

Paul wrote to a fearful, persecuted Church in Rome, and apparently he fielded many questions about what was to happen, who would be handed over, who would be condemned, and how things would turn out in the end. He did not respond with explanations or predictions but with the confident voice of hope:

> What will separate us from the love of Christ? Will anguish, or distress, or persecution, or famine, or nakedness, or peril, or the sword? . . . No, in all these things we conquer overwhelmingly through him who loved us. For I am convinced that neither death, nor life, nor angels, nor principalities, nor present things, nor future things, nor powers, nor height, nor depth, nor any other creature will be able to separate us from the love of God in Christ Jesus our Lord. (Rom 8:35, 37-39)

For those of us who preach the Word, "That's the way it is" and "It is what it is" mean much more than Cronkite or *USA Today* sports commentators intended. "The way it is" is much more expansive than what we see before us. Hoping in God, we entrust everything to his mysterious, hidden wisdom. Our experience of the groaning of creation and our subjection to futility does not have to paralyze us. We proclaim his Word and submit ourselves to it personally, for he sheds light on all who listen. We trust that though we do not understand everything, God does, and that's what matters. We look to the cross with hope in Christ who carried us there with him.

The Serenity Prayer is generally attributed to theologian Reinhold Niebuhr. Most of us have probably committed part of it to memory, but perhaps you have never seen the full prayer, which calls attention to God taking our fallen world "as it is."

> God grant me the serenity
> to accept the things I cannot change;
> courage to change the things I can;
> and wisdom to know the difference.
> Living one day at a time;
> Enjoying one moment at a time;
> Accepting hardships as the pathway to peace;
> Taking, as He did, this sinful world
> as it is, not as I would have it;
> Trusting that He will make all things right
> if I surrender to His Will;
> That I may be reasonably happy in this life
> and supremely happy with Him
> Forever in the next.
> Amen.

Sincerely in Christ,

+ Peter Sartain

Archbishop Peter Sartain

29

Mary, Mother of Priests

Dear Brothers in the Lord,

When the USCCB met in San Antonio in 2009, five large banners were displayed behind the platform where conference officers were seated. Each represented an apparition of the Blessed Mother to Hispanic people: Our Lady of Guadalupe (Mexico), Our Lady of Charity of Cobre (Cuba), Our Lady of Aparecida (Brazil), Our Lady of Divine Providence (Puerto Rico), and Our Lady of Mercy (Peru). The banners sent an important message to us bishops that the Virgin makes herself known in every land, through every culture.

Since I did not grow up in a Hispanic culture, my understanding of the Blessed Virgin's love for Hispanic people and their love for her was as an outsider, more historical or sociological than spiritual. But when I began to study the Spanish language and celebrate Mass and other devotions with Hispanic parishioners, I noticed beautiful things. The first was that people speak of Our Lady with terms of love and endearment. She is not only *Nuestra Señora*—she is also *Madrecita*, *La Virgencita*, and *La Morenita*. This striking familiarity taught me that the bond of love between Mary and Hispanic people is strong, warm, and trusting. One can go to *la Madrecita* with one's most intimate problems. One can say to her things one would never say to anyone else, and she listens with attentiveness and compassion.

Through the years, priestly ministry has helped me grow in devotion to Mary. Marian devotion was always strong in our home, and we often prayed the rosary as a family, but I did not nurture my relationship with her as I grew older. It was after ordination, in part through the example of parishioners and their spontaneous attraction to the suffering mother of Jesus, that I began to turn intentionally toward her myself. My first priestly assignment was to Our Lady of Sorrows Parish, and I think she took me under her wing then, though I did not realize it right away. Studying Scripture and theology and preaching about Mary have opened my eyes to her essential role in the Christian faith as well as her indispensable relationship to priests.

What strikes me about biblical depictions of Mary is that while they present her as a key figure, she is usually behind the scenes. Her presence is powerful, and nothing would have happened without her "yes." And yet she is quiet, meditating on the events of which she is a part but does not always understand.

The *Catechism of the Catholic Church* quotes Blessed John Henry Newman when explaining that revealed truths can seem obscure to human reason and experience. In his *Apologia pro vita sua*, Newman wrote: "Ten thousand difficulties do not make one doubt." In other words, it is natural to grapple with the difficulties and questions that those truths present to us. Still, faith is "more certain than all human knowledge because it is founded on the very word of God who cannot lie" (*Catechism* 157). Mary did not always understand what was happening, and her first impulse was to ask questions:

> But she was greatly troubled at what was said and pondered what sort of greeting this might be. (Luke 1:29)

> When his parents saw him they were astonished, and his mother said to him: "Son, why have you done this to us? Your father and I have been looking for you with great anxiety." (Luke 2:48)

The fact that she did not readily comprehend her place in God's plan makes her an even more approachable and, ironically, more heroic figure. For her lack of comprehension did not cause her to say "no" to God. Her faith allowed her to see through her difficulties to the fidelity of God, who cannot lie.

Mary is a creature, a believer, and a disciple like us. She is one who heard God's word and took it seriously. As Luke writes: "Mary kept all these things, reflecting on them in her heart" (Luke 2:19). She turned the word over and over within, seemingly without the urge to figure things out or neatly resolve them to her satisfaction. It was enough for her to know that the God who called her to experience them would in time make everything clear. She did not ask God to define her "place" or specify her "niche." It was enough for her to know that he was somehow using her and that everything would be resolved in his love. Her compassionate companionship with all Christians springs from her absolute trust in God, her personal experience of suffering and uncertainty, and her willingness to cooperate with God's grace even in obscurity.

It is interesting that in Luke Mary identifies herself as a "handmaid" while the angel's assessment of her is that she is "the favored one," the object of God's love. When Juan Diego told the Virgin he had been unsuccessful in relaying her message to the bishop, he suggested she send someone of greater stature. He explained, "Because for sure, I am a meager peasant, a cord, a little ladder, the people's dung; I am a leaf." But to Mary he was "Juan Diegito, the dearest of my children." Mary considered herself a "handmaid," but the angel told her she was the "favored one." Juan Diego considered himself "the people's dung," but Mary considered him "the dearest of my children."

In my teenage years, I lost the habit of praying the rosary; but after ordination I noticed how comforting it was to parishioners who lost a loved one and how it was the preferred prayer at almost every wake service. I took up the practice again, and it became part of my regimen of daily prayer. I'm not sure that I pray the rosary well, but I have come to understand that Mary uses it to show me her care and keep me close to Jesus. She is always saying to me, "Do whatever he tells you." She is always extending to me her motherly embrace.

Moreover, I have come to understand that my spiritual life as a priest would be incomplete without devotion to Mary. How could I ever ignore the one who is the "favored one" of God, the first and best disciple, the one who shows us the fruit of cooperating with grace? Again and again, I have seen parallels between our vocation to the priesthood *with its sole identity in Jesus* and the pattern of her life. I have found in the disorientation of transfer from parish to parish, diocese to diocese, that she offers assurance and peace. I have found that at times of unanswerable questioning she offers a steady hand. I have found that in times of discouragement, she reminds me who I am to God. I have found that when I hand over people and situations to her, she never lets me down. I have found that when trying to figure out how God is using me she helps me let go of the need to know. Seeking to follow her example, I have learned how difficult it is to say, simply, "Let it be done to me according to your word"—and follow through with generosity and humility.

Because Mary's meditating on "all these things" was not merely a pious compliance with what she did not understand, she is a great inspiration for preachers. The Mother of the Word Incarnate shows us how to let the Word enter our depths where it becomes the foundation of our thoughts and perspectives. The answer to our weekly question, "What will I preach about this Sunday?" will come much more easily if we not only spend time with the Lectionary but also make a habit of letting the Word dwell within as the very atmosphere we breathe and as the truth God desires to make incarnate in us.

Mary is a living symbol of what God wishes to do for us all. More than a symbol, however, she is our loving mother who lends us her ear and her heart, to whom we can go with our most difficult struggles. She is our intercessor, who goes to her Son with our prayer—and who takes us with her. She is an evangelizer who helps us understand and preach the Gospel she has pondered and lived fully. After all, it was her vocation to bear Christ and give him to the world! She is comfort in our suffering, because she has suffered herself and did not always understand what was happening to her. She is our companion wherever life takes us, and she is always happy to be at our side.

At the end of *I Will Give You Shepherds*, Blessed John Paul II writes that "Mary was called to educate the one eternal priest, who became docile and subject to her motherly authority" (82). Doesn't it make sense that she would extend that same motherly, priestly formation to us—and that we would receive it with the docility of her Son?

Many years ago, from among the premiums offered for having sold a certain quota of a product in his drug store, my father chose an eighteen-inch plaster of Paris statue of the Blessed Mother holding Jesus in her arms. It stood on the buffet in our dining room for as long as I can remember, and now it stands on the mantel in my living room. It takes me back to childhood (she was always there), but even more it reminds me of the devotion that anchored our family and was no doubt a central factor in my vocation. Whether we realize it or not, it is the same for all of us. She prays that everyone will listen to the voice of her Son.

Several times each day I ask the Blessed Mother to look after, protect, encourage, and inspire you. I have confidence that she does.

> Pray for us, O holy Mother of God, that our faith and courage may increase, that we will grow ever closer to your Son, and that the

Word you bore may take flesh in us. As it is for you, may everything about us be about him.

Sincerely in Christ,

+ *Peter Sartain*

Archbishop Peter Sartain

30

Proclaiming and Praying the Name of Jesus

Dear Brothers in the Lord,

Many years ago I began placing a pen and notepad on my nightstand and next to the chair where I pray in my chapel. Occasionally a thought will occur to me that I want to remember for a homily, a column, or a letter to you. But just as often I use the pen and paper to write myself a reminder to do something. If I say to myself, "I will remember that," I will either promptly forget it, be unable to sleep, or be distracted for the rest of my prayer in the attempt to remember it. If I write it down, however, I have preserved the thought and robbed it of its power to distract me.

Some days I seem to go from distraction to distraction. In fact, some days I simply seem to be more *distractable* than other days. Street noise, music, overheard conversations—just about anything—can distract me from the tasks at hand. Whether working or praying, at such times my mind wanders unchecked, and all of a sudden I realize that I have meandered far from the present moment. Thus pen and paper at strategic spots around the house.

I take consolation that the great St. Thomas Aquinas was also plagued by distraction. "It is hardly possible to say a single Our Father without our minds wandering off to other things," he writes. Furthermore and consolingly, "to wander in mind unintentionally does not deprive prayer of its fruit," and "it is not necessary that prayer should be attentive throughout, because the force of the original intention with which one begins prayer renders the whole prayer meritorious."[1]

It is not only individual tasks and prayer that are interrupted by distraction. In our case, ministry can be besieged by all manner of distraction: financial strain, conflict, scandal, temptation, sin, worry, staff problems, ambition, discouragement, capital projects, ideology, illness, anger, resentment, fatigue, and so on. The list is endless. At times we have an obligation to give such distractions direct attention in order to resolve or disarm them. But in certain instances, Satan would prefer that we not address them but be relentlessly harassed by them, because the mischief they work is a powerful obstacle to the mission of the Church.

Ironically, even while tending responsibly to the routine of ministry, we can lose focus without knowing it if, for example, simply "getting things done" becomes our lone goal. We can give so much energy and importance to a pet parish program (as good as it might be) that the program itself becomes "the point" of our day or "the point" of parish life. If "getting things done" or a single program becomes the point, it is quite possible that following Jesus is no longer the point. The routine, the program, have become a distraction.

> As they continued their journey he entered a village where a woman whose name was Martha welcomed him. She had a sister named Mary [who] sat beside the Lord at his feet listening to him speak. Martha, burdened with much serving, came to him and said, "Lord, do you not care that my sister has left me by myself to do the serving? Tell her to help me." The Lord said to her in reply, "Martha, Martha, you are anxious and worried about many things. There is need of only one thing. Mary has chosen the better part and it will not be taken from her." (Luke 10:38-42)

Though there is never a moment when we are not in the presence of the Lord Jesus, there might very well be moments when we are not present to him, when our minds and hearts have wandered, lured away by just about anything, "burdened with much serving." If we want to be good pastors, we will take care to see that he is literally and intentionally in our minds and in our hearts at all times. We will be vigilant to remind ourselves that he is always *before us* and we are to *follow*. Sitting at Jesus' feet, we will say his name often and listen to him speak.

Saying the name of Jesus intends more than speaking a word or repeating a theme. Speaking his name means proclaiming his power, submitting ourselves to his universal reign, and placing ourselves under his providential care. His is a powerful name, spiritually more powerful than we can possibly grasp. Paul writes to the Philippians:

> God greatly exalted him
>   and bestowed on him the name
>   that is above every name,
>   that at the name of Jesus
>   every knee should bend,
>   of those in heaven and on earth and under the earth,
>   and every tongue confess that
>   Jesus Christ is Lord,
>   to the glory of the Father. (Phil 2:9-11)

In *The Jesus Prayer,* Lev Gillet suggests that the Acts of the Apostles could be called "the book of the name of Jesus," for "In the name of Jesus the good news is preached, converts believe, baptism is conferred, cures and other signs are accomplished, lives are risked and given."[2] The name of Jesus was so powerfully connected to the ministry of the apostles that after being taken into custody for having cured a cripple in his name, Peter and John were eventually released by the Sanhedrin with a warning "never again to speak to anyone in this name" (Acts 4:17)—to which they replied, "It is impossible for us not to speak about what we have seen and heard" (4:20). It was not much later that the high priest was compelled to remind them, "We gave you strict orders [did we not?] to stop teaching in that name. Yet you have filled Jerusalem with your teaching" (5:28).

Perhaps it seems simplistic or pietistic to encourage you to speak the name of Jesus at all times, but nothing could be further from the truth. We need to be constantly alert to his presence, and our people need to hear us constantly proclaim Jesus as Lord. "There is no salvation through anyone else, nor is there any other name under heaven given to the human race by which we are to be saved" (Acts 4:12).

The name of Jesus should be on our lips in every homily, at every meeting, in every counseling session, at every moment of prayer. His name should be in every parish and school mission statement. As we go through the day, we should pray his name silently to remind ourselves of his nearness and seek his protection. In moments of transition from one appointment to another, we should pray the name of Jesus, who accompanies us to the next one. At times of confusion and anxiety, we should pray the name of Jesus, who calms every storm. At times of distraction, we should pray the name of Jesus, who brings recollection and order by his love. Philotheus, writing in the eighth or ninth century, suggests that the Jesus Prayer has power "to concentrate the scattered intellect."[3] At times of temptation, we should pray the name of Jesus, for Satan shudders at the hearing of his name and flees. Praying the name of Jesus, we take our place among the leprous and grieving, the blind and the lame, the sinful and the searching, who cried out to him for help.

Speaking and praying the name of Jesus is not some kind of magical incantation but implies a living relationship, a humble acknowledgment of his sovereignty, and an echo of the publican's prayer, "O God, be merciful to me, a sinner." The Jesus Prayer is a cry uttered in weakness, a desperate supplication rooted in total dependence on him, a plea voiced by a distracted heart, an honest recognition of our need for conversion, a grateful awareness that we live in his loving embrace, and a profession of faith that he is Lord, Savior, God. Praying and proclaiming the name of Jesus means committing oneself to do the will of the Father, as he did.

Thus praying the name of Jesus and committed discipleship go hand in hand.

> Not everyone who says to me, "Lord, Lord," will enter the kingdom of heaven, but only the one who does the will of my Father in heaven. Many will say to me on that day, "Lord, Lord, did we not prophesy in your name? Did we not drive out demons in your name? Did we not do mighty deeds in your name?" Then I will declare to them solemnly, "I never knew you. Depart from me, you evildoers." (Matt 7:21-23)

Paul proclaims, "for me, life is Christ." So it is with us: he is not the main topic of conversation; he is our life. Saint John Chrysostom writes,

> Do not estrange your heart from God, but abide in Him and always guard your heart by remembering our Lord Jesus Christ, until the name of the Lord becomes rooted in the heart and it ceases to think of anything else. May Christ be glorified in you.[4]

Will I follow the one whose name I call day and night? Will I let him teach me to do the Father's will, lead me, form me, correct me, forgive me, love me, be my all? Will I proclaim him even when his name meets rejection and ridicule? Will I risk the criticism that inevitably rises when I preach the folly of the cross? Can I honestly say that it is impossible for me not to speak of what I have seen and heard? In the face of all that will distract me and others, will I do all I can to make Jesus the focus of the rectory, the parish, the archdiocese?

To pray the name of Jesus, to go about ministry in his name, implies that our hearts are set on following him and him alone. Not to follow him, not to cling to him, would mean being without sail and rudder, literally driven to distraction by just about any wind that blows and wave that moves.

Lev Gillet also writes:

> To pronounce the name of Jesus in a holy way is an all-sufficient and surpassing aim for any human life. . . . We are to call to mind Jesus Christ until the name of the Lord penetrates our heart, descends to its very depths. . . . The name of Jesus, once it has become the center of our life, brings everything together.[5]

And the author of the Letter to the Hebrews reminds us:

> Therefore, since we are surrounded by so great a cloud of witnesses, let us rid ourselves of every burden and sin that clings to us and persevere in running the race that lies before us while keeping our eyes fixed on Jesus, the leader and perfecter of faith. (Heb 12:1-2)

When I was Bishop of Little Rock, a local psychologist and convert to the faith had the habit of writing periodic letters of prayer and encouragement to the circle of priests and deacons she knew. I was blessed to be on her list. One of those letters ended with the following prayer, one that I offer now for you:

Lord Jesus, give him faith
and trust that never waver,
even though
his feelings, his moods, fluctuate,
even though
circumstances change,
pain intrudes,
distraction allures,
weakness presents itself,
and noise and clamor
threaten to overwhelm

the stillness,

the silence

of You.

Be his peace, Lord Jesus.

Be his love, Lord Jesus.

Be his distraction, Lord Jesus.

Be his strength,

his faith,

his rest,

his passion,

his all.

Lord Jesus, be his very self,

that they too

may see You

in him.[6]

—Carol Siemon, PhD

Sincerely in Christ,

+ Peter Sartain

Archbishop Peter Sartain

Notes

1. Qtd. in Paul Murray, OP, *Praying with Confidence: Aquinas on the Lord's Prayer* (London: Continuum, 2010), 47–48.

2. A Monk of the Eastern Church (Lev Gillet), *The Jesus Prayer* (Crestwood, NY: St. Vladimir's Seminary Press, 1987), 27.

3. Ibid., 41n18.

4. Qtd. in Callistus and Ignatius, "*Directions to Hesychasts,*" in *Writings from the Philokalia on Prayer of the Heart,* translated by E. Kadloubovsky and G.E.H. Palmer (New York: Faber & Faber, 1995), 194.

5. A Monk of the Eastern Church, 41.

6. Poem by Carol Siemon, PhD. Used by permission.

31

They Would Like to See Jesus

Dear Brothers in the Lord,

She attended Sunday Mass at St. Peter Manor for just a few weeks, having arrived from nowhere by taxi. None of the residents knew who she was, and had they known they would have been quick to spread the word through the confining world of their seniors' residence. She was petite, well-dressed, reverent, and slightly bent with age. However, no one would sit next to her because, despite her dress and demeanor, her hygiene was terribly poor. I'm ashamed to say that I, too, noticed the unpleasant odor when she came to Communion, and part of me wanted to avoid her.

It was clear she wanted to be there, but she and the taxi driver must have agreed upon a tightly-fixed schedule, for just as suddenly as she appeared each Sunday, she disappeared as Mass ended. I was never able to speak with her and was always intrigued by her presence.

In *Novo Millennio Ineunte,* Blessed John Paul II recounts his experience of the Great Jubilee of 2000. In a moving reflection about watching pilgrims coming to Rome, he writes:

> I have been impressed this year by the crowds of people which have filled St. Peter's Square at the many celebrations. I have often

stopped to look at the long queues of pilgrims waiting patiently to go through the Holy Door. In each of them I tried to imagine the story of a life, made up of joys, worries, sufferings; the story of someone whom Christ had met and who, in dialogue with him, was setting out again on a journey of hope.

As I observed the continuous flow of pilgrims, I saw them as a kind of concrete image of the pilgrim Church, the Church placed, as Saint Augustine says, "amid the persecutions of the world and the consolations of God." We have only been able to observe the outer face of this unique event. Who can measure the marvels of grace wrought in human hearts? (8)

I saw the little lady who arrived at Mass by taxi only a handful of times. I witnessed the "outer face" of that unique event—*her* outer face—and I guessed at the story beneath. My guesses made me feel sorry for her, but at the same time I had no doubt there was some "marvel of grace" at work that brought her there, some hope, some encounter. I hope we did not repulse her with our discriminating noses. I hope she encountered Jesus in our midst.

Long ago, perhaps inspired by Blessed John Paul's account of the Jubilee pilgrims, I began purposely looking out over crowds at Mass and other gatherings. I began studying more attentively the faces of those who come forward for Holy Communion. What brings them? What stories would they tell? What's going on at home? How can I reach them? What does that expression on his face mean? Have I misread her? I have wondered at times whether in searching and studying faces I am allowing myself to be distracted, but that's not what happens. I won't be able to speak personally to everyone after Mass, but I will have seen them. I will have seen the outer face of the marvel of grace, the outer face of an interior encounter.

"Sir, we would like to see Jesus," the visiting Greek converts to Judaism said to Philip at Passover (John 12:21). At its most basic level, that is what our people say to us. No matter our ministry—parish, higher education, campus ministry, hospital chaplaincy—that is what those we encounter desire. "We would like to see Jesus," they say, and they count on us to take them to him.

I have a feeling many folks became annoyed the day the four friends of the paralyzed man carried him to Jesus (Luke 5:17-26; Mark 2:1-12). After all, they had arrived early where he was to preach, and sitting at the Teacher's feet was a privilege earned on a first-come, first-served basis. "Why didn't these latecomers arrive earlier, like we did?" they might have asked themselves. "Let them stand outside in the sun. His stretcher alone would take the space of three people."

Making themselves as comfortable as was possible in such cramped quarters, they listened to Jesus, only to have their attention interrupted by the grumbling of the crowd outside and the heavy thud of footsteps on the roof above. "What now?" they wondered, wishing the noise would stop, that these uninvited guests would go away. But the noise continued, and chunks of mud and straw began to fall from the ceiling as the roof itself was removed. People coughed and fumed, their annoyance growing by the second. Cramped became chaotic as to their own amazement they made room for a stretcher lowered clumsily to the floor.

As everyone's attention shifted from Jesus to the dust-filled air and the gutsy crippled man now on the floor, Jesus' attention shifted, too. Clear through the heavy air, he saw a man—a soul—with faith. "As for you, your sins are forgiven . . . I say to you, rise, pick up your stretcher, and go home" (Luke 5:20, 24). Everyone was amazed, astonished, struck with awe. "We have seen incredible things today" (v. 26).

Among the crowd were scribes and Pharisees, some of whom protested to themselves that Jesus blasphemed when he said, "Your sins are forgiven." Everyone knew that only God could forgive sins. But others present that day realized that God had indeed forgiven sins, had indeed healed a paralyzed man.

There was a further lesson. They had witnessed the extraordinary determination of one drawn irresistibly to Jesus, one who would let no barrier keep him away. No doubt about it, the paralytic had been healed—he left the place on his own two feet, carrying his stretcher and "glorifying God" —but the additional lesson was the attraction and the response. Four men had broken through the roof to lower their friend to Jesus—because their friend had sensed that in Jesus God himself had broken through to him. Faith is both a gift offered by God and a response returned by us—and he even inspires the response.

Matthew 8:5-13 recounts the time a Roman centurion, anxious for the health of his paralyzed servant but feeling unworthy of a visit from Jesus, approaches the Lord in Capernaum. Jesus immediately responds, "I will come and cure him," but the centurion declines, offering a surprisingly insightful profession of faith in the power and authority of Jesus' word.

> "Lord, I am not worthy to have you enter under my roof; only say the word and my servant will be healed. For I too am a person subject

to authority, with soldiers subject to me. And I say to one, 'Go,' and he goes; and to another 'Come here,' and he comes; and to my slave, 'Do this,' and he does it." (Matt 8:8-9)

"Amazed" at the centurion's faith, Jesus heals the servant "at that very hour."

Some came looking for Jesus, and simultaneously Jesus went looking for others.

> While the crowd was pressing in on Jesus and listening to the word of God, he was standing by the Lake of Gennesaret. He saw two boats there alongside the lake; the fishermen had disembarked and were washing their nets. Getting into one of the boats, the one belonging to Simon [Peter], he asked him to put out a short distance from the shore. Then he sat down and taught the crowds from the boat. (Luke 5:1-3)

Reading that pericope, I always stop for a moment to consider what it must have been like for Peter when Jesus came and sat in his boat. Had they even met before that day? I can picture Peter feverishly tidying up, hurling nets and needles and hooks to one side and out of the Lord's way. Since he had no warning, his boat was a smelly, oily mess, and sticky fish blood was everywhere. Was he annoyed, just for a moment, that Jesus had chosen his boat instead of the other?

Unconcerned about the mess, Jesus commandeered Peter's boat for his own purposes. Peter backed off and listened as Jesus began to teach the crowds. Listening again, hesitantly, when Jesus told him to lower his nets to the deep for a catch of fish, his life was changed forever. The Son of God had broken into Peter's boat because the crowds were pressing so hard against him. In choosing Peter's boat, he was actually choosing Peter. Peter made room not only in his cluttered boat but more importantly, in his life, surrendering *everything* to Jesus (even his doubt that Jesus could fish better than he, the professional!).

The paralyzed man would let nothing stop him from getting close to Jesus, so his friends broke through the roof. The centurion traveled to Capernaum to plead for his servant, trusting in Jesus' authoritative word. Jesus would let nothing stop him from teaching the crowds, so he hijacked Peter's boat. In every case, his disciples witness a marvel of grace, an encounter of Jesus with someone seeking him.

Every day it is the same with you and me. Our parishes, our schools, our towns are alive with this deepest dynamic of the human person: the desire to see Jesus. Some of those who come seeking him are "registered" seekers, but many are not. We know many of their names, but others are unknown to us. Some will come every Sunday, but others will arrive from nowhere only once, then disappear. In some cases, the dynamic has yet to awaken, for faith has yet to be given—some of those we see each day do not know Jesus. In other cases, the dynamic is real but submerged beneath religious observance that has become routine—they are there but might seem inattentive. In other cases, authentic faith is hidden beneath a veneer of suspicion and hurt— "Prove to me that he is real, that you are sincere," they seem to say. In others, they come in hope that *this* will be the day they encounter the Lord in a life-changing way—their hearts open, they wait for him. In still others, the dynamic is explicit, intentional, and profound—we marvel at their faith, depend on their prayers, and ask their help.

No matter how they look or seem, they are there to see Jesus. We are there to show them his face.

After once celebrating Mass for the Chinese Catholic Community, I was approached by an elderly woman who spoke very broken English. I understood little of what she said, but a member of the community explained that she wanted me to know she had arrived in the United States just two years ago after spending most of her life under Communist oppression. She moved to Seattle to be with her daughter and discovered on the internet that there is a Chinese Catholic Community here. For the first time in her life she can practice her faith openly, without fear. Now stricken with cancer, every Sunday she takes two buses to get to Mass.

We priests are just like the paralyzed man, like Peter, like the centurion and his slave. We are to go to any length necessary—asking others to carry us if need be—to spend time with the Lord ourselves. We are to allow our lives to be overtaken, overpowered, hijacked by him. We are to trust in the power of his Word, the Word that goes forth from our mouths and example to the ears and eyes of those who seek him. Moreover, in the Church, caught up and placed "amid the persecutions of the world and the consolations of God," we are to look with Jesus through the dust and debris, the baggage and distrust—and yes, sometimes the stench—and see *souls*: souls with faith strong and shaky, souls with faith yet to blossom, souls awaiting the gift. Perhaps they will arrive by taxi from nowhere or by bus from a world away. Among them we will see someone Christ has met or would like to meet, and who, in dialogue with him, will set out on a journey of hope. Among them we will see the face of Christ.

Whether we notice or not, we see incredible things every day.

Sincerely in Christ,

+ *Peter Sartain*

Archbishop Peter Sartain